BRITAIN IN OLD P

South Shropshire

DAVID TRUMPER

SUTTON PUBLISHING

Sutton Publishing Limited
Phoenix Mill · Thrupp · Stroud
Gloucestershire · GL5 2BU

First published 2001

Cover photographs: St Michael and All Angels' church, Lydbury North, *c.* 1925. Lydbury North was a thriving settlement long before Bishop's Castle was founded in the twelfth century. The church is a reminder of the village's more prosperous days. Standing in the middle of the village, its massive Norman tower dominates the surrounding area.

British Library Cataloguing in Publication Data
A catalogue record for this book is available from the British Library.

ISBN 0-7509-2785-2

Typeset in 10.5/13.5 Photina.
Typesetting and origination by
Sutton Publishing Limited.
Printed and bound in England by
J.H. Haynes & Co. Ltd, Sparkford.

*In loving memory of my grandparents,
Alice Laura and Richard Thomas Corfield,
who were both born in South Shropshire.*

Castle Street, Bishop's Castle, *c.* 1900. The Norman castle was built in about 1127, but very little remains as it became ruinous in the seventeenth century. A piece of the old castle wall can be seen from Castle Street and the motte is now a bowling green. Another part of the castle site is occupied by the Castle Hotel, which was built in about 1719.

CONTENTS

Ludlow Town Hall, 21 March 1986. The demolition of the old Victorian town hall is well under way. The site has not been built on but has been incorporated into the open market area in front of the castle. Shortly before it was demolished it was used for scenes in the BBC Two series *Blott on the Landscape*, which was filmed in and around Ludlow.

Hopesay, *c.* 1930. The tiny settlement of Hopesay lies in a valley surrounded by the Aston, Burrow, Hopesay and Wart Hills. There are prehistoric hill forts on the Barrow and the Wart. The name is derived from 'hop', a valley, and 'say', from the de Say family. In the village there are a number of fine Victorian houses with some beautifully matured gardens. The oldest house is Hopesay Farmhouse, which was built of stone with some later timber-framed additions.

INTRODUCTION

The area featured in this book is mainly within the boundaries served by the South Shropshire town and parish councils. It is a land created by the actions of many generations and an area of contrasting and outstanding beauty. Bordering Herefordshire, Worcestershire and Wales, this region has seen great turmoil in the past, as its ruined castles and fortifications will testify.

In about AD 790 a great dyke was built by Offa, King of Mercia, to form a border between the English and Welsh-speaking peoples. After the Norman Conquest a line of castles was erected along the border to stop Welsh incursions into Shropshire and from which counter-attacks could be launched. At first the defence of the border was under the control of Roger de Montgomery, the first Earl of Shrewsbury, but after one of his sons rebelled against King Henry I in 1102, authority for the area reverted back to the Crown. In the fifteenth century the Council of the Marches was introduced to control affairs along the border. Its headquarters were at Ludlow Castle and it ruled for two centuries until it was abolished in 1689. The remains of many castles and large stretches of Offa's Dyke can still be seen to remind us of those more turbulent days.

Over the centuries the area has sunk into quiet obscurity, prompting A.E. Housman to write:

> In valley of springs and rivers,
> By Onny, Teme and Clun,
> The country for easy livers,
> The quietest under the sun.

It is a land containing a huge variety of scenery, rich fertile valleys, open barren moor and heathland, undulating foothills to the heights of the Long Mynd, the boulder-strewn Stiperstones and the Clee Hills reaching up to over 1,800 ft above sea level.

The hills of Stretton and the Stiperstones are formed out of the ancient pre-Cambrian rocks while the Clee Hills to the south are sandstone, capped with dolerite or Dhu-stone, the local black rock. This area like the Stiperstones has been ravaged over the years by quarrying and mining. To the east of the Clee Hills is the Wyre Forest, while in the south-west are the remains of the old Clun Forest, parts of which reach into Wales.

There are numerous habitations, from the timber-framed and stone villages and hamlets nestling in quiet secluded valleys, to the small scattered farmsteads, some with the remains of moats and other fortifications, dating back to the middle ages.

There are the grand houses and estates, some like Whitton Court and Plowden Hall, built over several hundred years, to Downton Castle and Stokesay Court, erected by rich industrialists in the eighteenth and nineteenth centuries.

Finally there are the small market towns of Cleobury Mortimer, Clun, Church Stretton, Bishop's Castle, Craven Arms and Ludlow, which was described as 'the finest small town in the whole of England'. All are full of charm, packed with architecture of every style and date and brimming with history.

Whitton Court, 27 June 1965. This mansion incorporates part of the fourteenth-century stone hall, and has a timber-framed annexe; in the Tudor period was faced with brick. The court was the home of the Charlton family for several generations. Inside there are some fine wall paintings dating from 1682, and over the fireplace is an excellent eighteenth-century hunting scene.

1

Stretton Dale

All Stretton, *c.* 1930. The village lies north-east of Church Stretton, between the Long Mynd on the west and Caer Caradoc to the east. Stretton is derived from 'Street Town', but according to local folklore King Charles II named the three settlements. Arriving at Little Stretton the king enquired his whereabouts, 'At Stretton if you please', replied a countryman. 'Little Stretton is a fitter name for so small a place', said the king and rode on towards Shrewsbury. On reaching the next village he again asked where he was. 'At Stretton', someone answered. Seeing the parish church whose bells were ringing in the old grey steeple, his majesty exclaimed, 'call it Church Stretton', and went on his way once more. Finally the king approached the next village and was again informed he was at Stretton. 'Stretton!' cried Charles in astonishment, 'why it's all Stretton about here!'

Yew Tree Inn, All Stretton, *c.* 1910. The Yew Tree seems to have been purpose built as an inn and dates from around 1620. In 1851 the landlord was William Hyde; to supplement his earnings he was also a cattle dealer. From around 1880 until the early 1920s the All Stretton Water Works Co. Ltd had their registered office at the inn. Mrs Seymour of Noel House Salisbury owned the inn in 1896, but by 1901 ownership had passed on to F. Cooper & Co., brewers from Burton-on-Trent.

The Village Shop, All Stretton, *c.* 1910. Early records show that John Rawlins owned the shop and Stores Cottage in 1849. When it was sold to Samuel Heighway in 1899 the property was described as 'a dwelling house, shop, outbuildings and garden'. He was particularly proud of his Indian and Ceylon teas, which he sold at 1*s* 10*d* or 2*s* a pound. In an advert he claimed customers for his tea from 'all over England including London, also Paris, Dresden and Munich'. Mr Heighway sold the business in 1922 to Edward Davies who in turn sold it to William Green two years later. Mr Green advertised in 1937 as a family grocer, provision, wine and spirit merchant. The family ran the store until 1968.

All Stretton Hall, June 1968. The hall, erected in about 1800, has a hipped roof and is built of brick with stone dressing. It became a hotel in the 1920s. In a 1928 advert its accommodation included a lounge hall, drawing room, smoking room, panelled oak dining room, excellent bedrooms and bathroom. They also boasted electric light, central heating, a garage and two tennis courts. The hotel was also supplied with fresh produce from its own large kitchen garden. The outdoor swimming pool is no longer a feature. This building has also got a number of wooden panels from the old hall.

The Church of St Michael and All Angels, All Stretton, *c.* 1910. At the beginning of the twentieth century the area around Church Stretton was becoming popular as a holiday resort and a residential area. New churches were needed; this one was consecrated on 24 October 1902. The money for the church was raised by the Revd R.C. Noel Hill, the rector, partly from the parish and partly from friends outside the parish. The building was designed by the Diocesan architect Mr Lloyd Oswell, and consists of a small apsed chancel, nave, south transept, bell tower and porch. It is built out of locally quarried Long Mynd stone with Grinshill stone dressing.

The Manor House, All Stretton, *c.* 1900. Part of the timber-framed building dates from about 1600. For a time in the early nineteenth century it became a maltings, but was later used as a lodging house for tramps and was licensed to sleep thirteen men, who had to spend the night standing up with their arms over a rope strung across the room. They were woken in the morning by the owner, who untied one end of the rope. No food was supplied, but any traveller who brought his own was allowed to warm it over the open fire. On the wall hung the following rules: 'No drink allowed on the premises. No bad language to be used. No drums to be used here. No washing on Saturday or Sunday. No smoking upstairs. Couples to wash their own pots.' At the beginning of the twentieth century the house was restored and was called the Manor House for the first time.

Cwm Spring Mineral Waters, All Stretton, *c.* 1910. The Stretton Hills Mineral Water Co. opened a factory on the Shrewsbury Road in 1883. It became one of the area's main employers and was known locally as the 'Pop Works'. Jewsbury & Brown ran it for many years until it was taken over by Wells' Drinks of Tenbury Wells. At the beginning of the twentieth century Francis Sutton FCS, FIC wrote, 'This is one of the purest waters which has ever come to my notice.' Dr W.D. Thursfield, the Medical Officer of Health for Shropshire, wrote, 'For gouty people the water of Cwm Dale is especially suited.'

High Street, Church Stretton, *c.* 1900. The photographs on this page show the same view but were taken almost half a century apart. The monument on the right was a drinking fountain erected to commemorate Queen Victoria's Diamond Jubilee in 1897. It was moved just a few years later to a site in front of Burway House where it remained until 1963, when it was taken down after a large vehicle had hit it, displacing the upper half. The plinth was demolished but the top section was 'stored', under a hedge in the town's cemetery, where it was recently discovered. The buildings on both corners of the road have also been demolished.

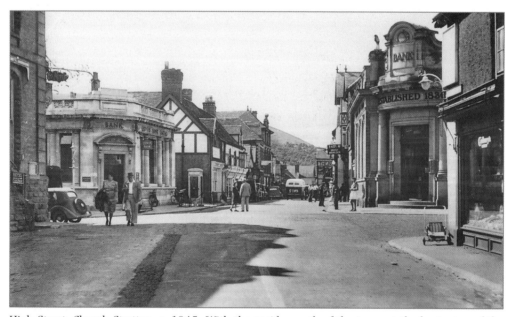

High Street, Church Stretton, *c.* 1945. With the rapid growth of the town at the beginning of the twentieth century banks were keen to get established in the town. On the left is Lloyds Bank and on the right is the Midland Bank, built on the site once occupied by the drinking fountain. Both banks were erected in the early 1920s. Note the white telephone box by Lloyds Bank.

The Hotel, Church Stretton, *c.* 1910. Stretton's most central hotel was built in three phases on the site of a farmhouse, an inn and a malt house. The first phase on the corner in 1861 replaced the Crown Inn and malt house. The second phase on Sandford Avenue was built in 1899, and the final phase along the Shrewsbury Road on the site of the farmhouse was completed in 1906. An inscribed stone from the old malt house has been retained. It reads, 'Erected by Copper A W his sonne Ano Dni 1587.'

The Hotel, Church Stretton, *c.* 1905. This is the rear of The Hotel showing 'the attractive Sun Parlour overlooking the garden and hills'. In the 1950s it was advertised as 'A House of Comfort and Courtesy'. It was fully licensed and open all year round with special terms for the winter season. The garden contained a croquet lawn, tennis courts and a bowling green.

The hotel fire, Church Stretton, 2 April 1968. The manageress raised the alarm after hearing an explosion in the reception area. Strong winds fanned the flames that spread at an alarming rate, filling the building with dense, black smoke. Forty firemen from around the county fought the blaze, their main priority being the trapped guests in the upper rooms. Several were rescued by ladder, including a young family from Stockport who were moving next day into a new home in Stretton. Both parents were brought out alive but the smoke suffocated their three sons. Two of the hotel staff also died in the fire: a waitress and a chambermaid.

The hotel fire, Church Stretton, 2 April 1968. The firemen took around half an hour to get the blaze under control but by then the roof and a great deal of the interior of the building had been destroyed. Frank Harbidge, Shropshire's Chief Fire Prevention Officer, said that if the recommended fire alarm had been in place lives would have been saved. In one bedroom Mr Harbidge had found a sign over a wash basin which read, 'In case of fire shout Fire', which he felt was unsatisfactory. A memorial to the victims can be found in St Lawrence's Church. The building has since been broken into smaller units that include flats, shops and a public house.

Sandford Avenue, Church Stretton, *c.* 1910. The avenue takes its name from the Revd Holland Sandford, rector of Eaton-under-Haywood. It was formerly known as Station Road and is the principal shopping area of the town. The shop with the clock over the door was one of the first plots to be developed on this road. It was occupied by Thomas Rich, a watchmaker and cycle dealer. He was responsible for the clock but after he left it fell into disrepair. It was restored with the aid of the town's Civic Society some years later.

Sandford Avenue, Church Stretton, *c.* 1905. This is a view looking the opposite way to the last photograph. On the left is the old post office building. It was later occupied by George Dunn, a dispensing chemist, who also ran a stationery and fancy goods repository and a circulating library. The building on the corner of Easthope Road is the old maltings. During the Second World War part of it was used as a workshop by the men of St Dunstan's. It is now an antique market.

Church Stretton station, *c.* 1958. The station stands on the main Shrewsbury to Hereford line and was opened in 1852. The old station buildings still stand on the other side of the bridge. This station to the south of the bridge was developed just before the First World War when the length of the platforms was increased. The station was modernised in February 1970 with the loss of a great deal of GWR-designed architecture. The engine is a Patriot Class called *St Dunstan*. It came into service in 1912 and was rebuilt in 1930.

Crossways, Church Stretton, *c.* 1960. Tower Buildings were the only shops to be completed from the Crossways Development Plan of 1905, when it was hoped to move the main shopping area away from the High Street to an area near the railway station. The architect used a design similar to the 'Rows' in Chester. The complex was demolished in 1965 for a traffic island that was never built. The part of the building with the domed roof was saved, and has been erected in a garden in the area as a summerhouse.

Broad Meadow Park, Church Stretton, *c.* 1925. The recreation ground was given to the Urban District Council by Ralph Benson, who had sold a large parcel of land in the town in about 1900 to be opened up as building plots. The park was enlarged by a gift of land from the Barn Owls, a local amateur dramatics group, who met in a converted barn. The park contains a bowling green, tennis courts and a children's play area. The entrance gates are the work of the Belgian wrought-iron artist M. Herman, who lived in the town as a refugee during the First World War.

Church Parade, Church Stretton, July 1909. Several times a year the army assembled at the camping ground just to the north of the town. This message was written on the reverse of the card: 'This was taken last Sunday morning on the camping ground. We (Grace and I) were standing more to the left so didn't get included in the group (thank goodness!). The Revd and Miss Osman have gone up to London until Saturday.' I presume that Mr Osman is conducting the service.

The Denehurst Hotel, Church Stretton, *c.* 1960. The Denehurst was built as a private house and was occupied in 1905 by Mrs Jones. In 1921 it was a boarding house run by Leonard Jones, and by 1928 it was advertised as a private hotel under the management of Mr and Mrs Barron. The hotel was always popular and in recent times hosted cabaret dinners where many top stars performed. In about 1990 a leisure centre was opened with a swimming pool, sauna, jacuzzi, gymnasium and solarium. The hotel will probably be demolished in 2001 and houses built on the site.

The Sandford Hotel, Church Stretton, *c.* 1960. At the beginning of the twentieth century Mrs Harriet Hardy ran the Sandford House Boarding Establishment and at that time the tariff was 5*s* 6*d* or 8*s* per day according to the season. This establishment also had links with the Stretton Boarding House by the North Pier in Blackpool. By 1921 her son Charles had upgraded it to a private hotel. It was an unlicensed premises until January 1948 when the Plough Inn closed in the High Street, and its licence transferred to the Sandford. The hotel closed in the 1980s and is now a nursing home.

Burway House, Church Stretton, *c.* 1900. Thomas Bridgman founded Burway House Free School in 1778. He left a charity of 40*s* a year to pay a schoolmaster to teach four poor children, 'til they could perfectly read the Bible'. When the elementary school opened in 1861 Burway House became the home of Samuel Harley Hough, a solicitor. At the beginning of the twentieth century it became a boys' boarding school, known as the Collegiate School. It then became a dentist's surgery and has since been changed into flats.

The Church Stretton Posting Establishment Ltd, *c.* 1900. The Hyslop family started the business in the nineteenth century. In 1895 David Hyslop advertised as a jobbing master, licensed to let post horses; he was also a coal merchant. By 1928 the car had replaced the horse and the business became known as the Central Garage, adapting many of the old buildings to suit their new business. They were advertised as motor engineers and railway carting agents, who were prepared to undertake all overhauls and repairs. They were also agents for the RAC and an appointed garage for the AA. A warning advised customers that cars would only be driven by staff at the owners' risk!

High Street, Church Stretton, *c.* 1905. This is a view of the street looking north towards the hotel. The stone building on the left is the Town Hall and Market, built in 1839 for £1,000 on the site of the old timber-framed market. The white building is the Plough Inn, which was first recorded in the eighteenth century. The inn once had a malt house next door where beer was brewed. It was delicensed in January 1948 and its licence transferred to the Sandford Hotel. The building on the right is Salt's ironmonger's shop with a fine frontage, built out of Ruabon brick, which was added in 1901. The building above is the Central Boarding House and Hotel (see page 22).

High Street, Church Stretton, *c.* 1905.
This is a better view of the town hall and
market, looking south. The traders sold
their wares beneath the arches, while the
business of the town was conducted in the
room above. The upper storey was also
used for concerts and public meetings and
had a capacity of around 250. In 1869
fortnightly penny readings took place
there for the benefit of the working
classes. It was a square building of red
brick with a stone dressing, supported on
stone pillars. A contemporary account
considered the building as 'neither
beautiful to the eye or with any
pretensions to architectural excellence'. It
was demolished in 1958 after it was found
to be unsafe.

The Raven Inn, Church Stretton, *c.* 1923. The Raven has been a public house since the early
eighteenth century and occupied buildings once belonging to the Bright family of Little Stretton.
It was delicensed in the 1970s. The newsagents belonged to Holmes and Jackson. As well as the
usual papers and magazines, they also had their own lending library and were the sole agents for
Sunday and evening newspapers. In the 1920s they took on the role of tourist information office,
advertising that they were 'pleased to assist with information about trains, charabanc tours,
historical places, favourite walks or entertainment'.

Boulton's shop, Church Stretton, *c.* 1925. Harry Boulton was a fishmonger and poultry dealer. He started his business in Sandford Avenue some time after 1905, but had moved to this shop in the High Street by 1921. He is seen here with his staff and transport, two bikes and a bull-nosed Morris van that delivered goods all around the area. This handsome display of poultry hanging outside the shop would be banned today under health and safety regulations. From left to right: -?-, Harry Boulton, George Lucas, Bob Boulton, Walter Bland.

The Central Boarding House and Hotel, Church Stretton, *c.* 1900. This building was erected in a narrow opening at the beginning of the eighteenth century and is a fine example of a Queen Anne house. In 1898 it was bought by Henry Rawlings for £1,000 and run as a hotel by his wife Frances. A guide for 1905 claims the hotel comes 'highly recommended for apartments, parties supplied, hot dinners and teas daily, good accommodation for cyclists, good stabling'.

St Lawrence's church, Church Stretton, *c.* 1930. Parts of the church date back to Norman times. The tower is late fifteenth to early sixteenth century and contains eight bells, six cast by Abraham Rudhall in 1711 and two more added later. The chiming clock was a gift from the rector, the Revd C. Noel Hill in 1890. This message to bell ringers was placed in the belfry in 1773: 'If you ring and do come here, You must ring well with hand and ear, And if the bell you overthrow, 4*d* to pay before you go, And if you ring in spur or hat, 6*d* you must pay for that, or in this place you swear and curse, 12*d* to pay pull out your purse.'

Church Street, Church Stretton, *c.* 1925. Church Street was once known as Back Lane. The Elementary School was built for £1,500, which was raised by public subscription. It was opened in January 1861 with three classrooms and was expected to take up to 144 children. The school was the first neo-timbered building to be erected in the town. A headmaster's house was also built with a garden and a pigsty. The school moved to new premises on the Shrewsbury Road in 1967; the old school is now the library and information centre.

Church Stretton Elementary School, *c.* 1910. Back row, left to right: Edith Tipton, Midge Pugh, -?-, -?-, William Tipton, -?-, Stan Robinson, -?-, Mr Butler, -?-. Third row: -?-, Doris Poole, Lucy Poole, -?-, -?-, Edith Lewis, -?-, -?-, Leonard Griffith, -?-, ? Clarke, -?-, -?-. Second row: -?-, Dick Tipton, ? Bebbington, Arthur Tipton, Mary Lewis, -?-, -?-, Fred Griffith, -?-, -?-, -?-. Front row: -?-, -?-, Ewart ?, Harold ?, Mac Price, Vincent Payne, Tom Poole, -?-.

Duke of Edinburgh Awards, Church Stretton, *c.* 1965. Two respected headmasters, Mr R. Morris (left) from Church Stretton Primary School and Mr R. Tanswell (right) from Church Stretton Secondary Modern School, present silver medal awards to four Ranger Guides. The guides are, left to right, Carol Edwards, Linda Owen, Shane Stephens and Vanessa Thomas.

Church Stretton Amateur Football Club, 1921. The season of 1920/21 proved a successful one for the club as they won both the Leintwardine Cup and the Church Stretton Infirmary Cup. Back row, left to right: P. Jones (Committee), H. Jones, F. Adlard, P. Catlow, W. Pierce, W. Bland, H. Humphreys (Hon. Sec.). Middle row: G. Jones, A. Pierce (Vice Capt.), W. Bailey, R. Keenan (Reserve). Front row: W. Brindley, J. Lewis (Capt.), H. Boulton, -?- (Mascot), F. Adlard, W. Humphries, R. Gillard (Reserve).

Church Stretton Football Club, c. 1960. The Church Stretton team pose proudly with the Shrewsbury League Runners-up Cup, presented by Alderman Sam Powell at the Gay Meadow, Shrewsbury. They lost 2-0 to Belle Vue in what Alderman Powell described as ' one of the best and most sporting junior games I have ever seen'. It was an even game but Stretton had the handicap of playing with ten men, when their captain went off in the seventh minute with a cut eye. A fine display of defending was given by Stretton's centre-half Fewtrell and goalkeeper Ray Tipton. The Stretton team were Ray Tipton, Reece, Lockley, Davies, Fewtrell, Coles (captain), Goode, Bearsley, Stone, Shut, P. Cole. Stretton had already won the Shrewsbury League Championship Trophy.

The Burway, Church Stretton, *c.* 1900. The Burway was once called Brook Street. The name recalls an open brook that ran from Prill Cottage to Sandford Avenue. This caused such severe flooding after heavy rain in the nineteenth century that Sandford Avenue was known as Lake Lane. The man with the horse and cart is the local refuse collector.

The Urban District Council, Church Stretton, March 1966. This photograph was taken at the last meeting of the Urban District Council, which was held in the Council Chamber in Beaumont Road. Seated, left to right: J.G. McMitchell, J.A. Russell, H.A. Horrocks, Dr McLintock, J.G. Tildesley (Chairman), J. Woolley, V.G.B. Mansell, Col. J.E. Russell, T.J. Black, J. Pryce-Jones. Standing: H.J.B. Williams (Clerk to Stretton UDC), G. Kellett (Treasurer to Ludlow RDC), E. Shaw (Engineer to Ludlow RDC), -?-.

The King's Arms, Church Stretton, *c.* 1910. In the past the High Street was known as the Bristol Road. The King's Arms on the right is in a building that dates back to the early seventeenth century and was probably built after the disastrous town fire of 1593. It was one of several public houses on the High Street. In his guide of Stretton in 1869, James Phillips thought that 'The Plough, Lion and King's Arms provide limited accommodation'.

Opposite, above: Little Stretton, *c.* 1925. This is a general view of the village, across the railway line to the Long Mynd. The area covered 4,743 acres and in 1911 the population was 309. In 1900 Edward Gibbon was the biggest landowner in the village; he lived at the Manor. Close to the village is the site of Brockhurst Castle, but little now remains of this large motte-and-bailey castle.

Opposite, below: Little Stretton, *c.* 1920. Customers pose outside one of the village shops. At this time there were three shops in Little Stretton. One was run by James Keenan, another by Harriet Lewis and the third by Edwin Evans who also kept the village post office.

The Old Tan House, Little Stretton, *c.* 1920. The house dates from the seventeenth century and was once the home of Derwent Wood, the sculptor, who was responsible for much of the restoration work. In 1921 Capt. D.E. Macpherson, a local pig breeder was in residence there. Unfortunately the flamboyant thatched entrance porch has disappeared.

The Ragleth Inn, Little Stretton, *c.* 1935. In 1900 there were three inns in the village, the Green Dragon, the Sun and the Crown. The Crown closed and was converted into the village shop. The Green Dragon is still in existence but the Sun has changed its name to the Ragleth, commemorating the hill near by. The sign outside the inn reads, 'Luncheons, Teas, Board Residence'. The cottages on the left are still called The Ancient House.

All Saints' Church, Little Stretton, *c.* 1920. This church was erected and paid for by Mrs Gibbon from the Manor House and was opened on 20 October 1903. It is an iron structure, ornamented in wood to give it a timber-framed appearance. It was bought from a firm in Manchester specialising in this type of building and was assembled by local workmen. A thatched roof was added in 1935, paid for by Derwent Wood from the Old Tan House, gives it a more rustic appearance.

Cardington, August 1961. Cardington is an attractive little village, built mainly of stone, 3½ miles north-east of Church Stretton. Behind the Royal Oak is the church of St James. The nave is Norman and up to 800 years old, while the tower is a mixture of early English and perpendicular styles. Inside is a handsome memorial to Judge William Leighton, the Chief Justice, who lived nearby at Plaish Hall. He died in 1607.

The Royal Oak, Cardington, June 1954. The inn is reputed to be one of the oldest in England. In 1901 the owner was Henry Reddin, a grocer, bootseller and wine and spirit merchant from Church Stretton. The interior has been heavily restored and modernised over the years. This photograph was taken by Jim Savage and includes his wife Pat and Mr and Mrs Chesterton.

Rushbury station, *c.* 1910. The station was on the Great Western Railway line that formed a direct route from Wellington to Craven Arms, via Much Wenlock. The line also had stops at Buildwas, Presthope and Longville. Passenger and freight services stopped in the 1950s and the line was lifted. The old station was then converted into a private house.

Ticklerton Court, *c.* 1910. Ticklerton was named in the Domesday Survey as Tickleworde and in later times as Tickleworthin. The court was the home of the Buddicom family for many years. William Buddicom who lived there in 1748, owned a small but beautifully carved Pilgrim's Cross, reputed to contain a fragment of the true cross.

Miss Fanny Jones' Tea Place, Chelmick, 21 September 1954. The tearoom at Chelmick near Hope Bowdler was a Mecca for hikers and walkers in the Stretton Hills. Miss Jones, shown here, ran the tea room with her sisters Sarah and Mary Ellen. The café opened just before the First World War and was in operation until 1955 when a fire burnt down the cottage. Visitors still remember the wonderful teas spread before them, with up to twenty-four varieties of home-made cake. The beautiful wisteria is thought to have been grown from a cutting from a tree at the Boathouse in Shrewsbury. It survived the fire and grew up the building that replaced the cottage.

2

The Long Mynd

The Long Mynd, 12 July 1965. In 1964 the National Trust launched a public appeal for £18,500 to buy 4,500 acres of the Long Mynd – aiming to preserve it as an area where the public could walk and enjoy the freedom of the open countryside. The appeal was a success and in less than a year the money was raised. This informal ceremony took place near the summit of the 1,700 ft range when Miss D.G. Outlaw, secretary of the Wolverhampton Centre, handed over the title deeds of the hills to John Cadbury, the president of the appeals committee that raised the money to buy the land.

The Long Mynd, July 1953. This photograph was taken near to the Boiling Well, which is close to Pole Hill, the summit of the Long Mynd, rising to a height of 1,700 ft above sea level. The hills are very ancient and were formed in the pre-Cambrian period. Although a beautiful tract of land in the summer, the hills have a bad reputation for taking men's lives in stormy weather. Such names as the Deadman's Hollow, the Devil's Mouth and Deadman's Beach are all ominous reminders of such events.

The Long Mynd, c. 1950. As well as driving or walking through the hills, another enjoyable way to find the more inaccessible places is on horseback. The Midland Trekking Centre at the Malthouse Stables, All Stretton, organised weeklong pony trekking holidays in the 1950s for just 13 guineas, which included your accommodation. Gliding first took place on the Long Mynd in 1934, and a club was established two years later in 1936.

The Long Mynd Hotel, *c.* 1899. In late Victorian times Church Stretton grew into a holiday and retirement spa. Because of its location in the heart of the Shropshire hill country it became known as Little Switzerland, the British Shangri-la or the Highlands of England. It boasted that it was strongly recommended by the medical profession for its 'magnificent scenery, pure air and water and equable climate'. The builders are posing in front of the shell of the new hotel that was opened in 1900.

The Long Mynd Hotel, *c.* 1905. The hotel is perched high on the side of the hill, around 850 ft above sea level. It was built by the Church Stretton Hydropathic Syndicate, and was originally called The Hydro Hotel. It was listed in 1900 as a first-class family and residential hotel set in 12 acres of beautifully wooded grounds. Its facilities included Turkish, medical and other baths. It also offered billiards, tennis, croquet and golf, or hunting with four packs of hounds.

Cardingmill Valley, 22 May 1961. This valley has attracted visitors for many years, especially in the late 1950s and early 1960s. At weekends hundreds of visitors from all over Shropshire and the Midlands would descend upon the valley for a pleasant day out. For the active there were walks up to the Light Spout Waterfall, to Mott's Road or to the ancient Bodbury Ring. For the less energetic a quiet picnic by the stream or an ice cream and a cup of tea at the Chalet Pavilion were pleasant ways to spend an afternoon.

Opposite, above: Trevor Hill, *c.* 1900. By the 1890s all available accommodation in the area was taken, especially during the summer months, but no new properties were being built. In 1896 a considerable amount of land for building was purchased by the Church Stretton Land Company, who did much to develop the area over the next few years. One of the first developments was on Trevor Hill. The building of the roads and houses left the side of the hill looking scarred and unattractive, but thankfully the first residents had enough foresight to plant trees and landscape the area. The building at the top is the golf club.

Opposite, below: Church Stretton Golf Club, *c.* 1910. The golf course was opened by Vardon and Taylor in 1898 and is situated on the eastern side of the lower slopes of the Long Mynd. The height of the course varies between 800 ft and 1,000 ft. In 1905 gentlemen residents of Stretton paid an annual subscription of 2 guineas; non-residents and ladies paid 1 guinea. Visitors' fees were *2s 6d* for one day, *7s 6d* for a week or *20s* for a month. A special discount of half fees was given to all members of the same family after the first two.

Cardingmill Valley, 1912. On a hot summer's day the old mill pool in the valley attracted local boys for swimming, but the facilities were hardly likely to attract the more genteel visitor. There was not much privacy for changing and the shed provided looks in need of renovation. Watching the bathers are Gordon Jones, sitting on the right bank, and his father on the horse.

Cardingmill Valley, 25 May 1959. By the 1950s only the brave or the foolhardy would swim in the pool and then they had to share it with thousands of tadpoles in the early spring. Sailing a boat was much more fun, though quite often you would have to wade in to retrieve your boat. The boys on the left are standing on the diving step. The pool was drained in the early 1960s and the site is now a car park, though you can still see the diving step and a notice stating a depth of 3 ft.

The Old Mill, Cardingmill Valley, *c.* 1900. The waters of the valley have been used to turn the wheel of the corn mill since medieval times. At the beginning of the nineteenth century a new mill was built as a carding mill for wool. In 1824 George Corfield built this three-storey building and installed spinning jennies and handlooms. In 1841 the building was known as Brooks Mill and there were forty-one people living and working there. As work at the mill dwindled the building was put to other uses. In 1881 a soda water and ginger beer manufacturer occupied part of the premises, while another part was used for accommodating visitors and as a tearoom. Part of the mill was demolished in 1912, but a large section of the factory has been converted into dwellings.

The Chalet Pavilion, Cardingmill Valley, *c.* 1930. The pavilion was made in sections and imported from Scandinavia. It closed during the Second World War but reopened in 1947, when they advertised that 'Every type of meal is supplied. Morning coffee, hot and cold lunches, meat teas or just a pot of tea and cake. Seats 250 and is a favourite rendezvous for works outings, social and sports clubs and Sunday school parties.' The National Trust bought the pavilion in 1978 and the tradition of warm hospitality to walkers and ramblers has continued.

Ashes Valley, Little Stretton, *c.* 1910. On the opposite side of Nils Hill is Ashes Hollow. This valley, with its picturesque slopes and winding track beside a gurgling brook, is gentler than Cardingmill Valley. It also gives the hiker a good walk up to Boiling Well and back to Church Stretton via the Townbrook Valley.

3

Craven Arms
& Corvedale

The Craven Arms Hotel, *c.* 1910. The hotel was built on land belonging to the Earl of Craven and was licensed in about 1810. It stands at a crossroads with Shrewsbury to the north, Ludlow and Hereford to the south, Clun to the west and Wenlock and Bridgnorth to the east. It was described in 1851 as a 'handsome and commodious hotel, not surpassed by any in the country'. By 1901 the accommodation consisted of a kitchen, tap room, smoke room, bar, coffee room, dining room, fifteen bedrooms and stabling for thirty horses. The landlord in 1901 was William Hide, and it's reported he kept the hotel clean and in good repair.

Craven Arms station, *c.* 1920. The railway between Shrewsbury and Ludlow was formally opened on 21 April 1852. The *Eddowes Journal* described Craven Arms' station as a 'large and commodious station, in the Elizabethan style of architecture, with pointed gables, a large booking office, ladies' and gentlemen's waiting rooms, an excellent residence, railway and road weighing machines, sidings, turntables and platform of 170 ft in length, cattle landing 200 ft, goods warehouse 80 ft by 40, coal wharf etc.' The first stationmaster was Mr Walker.

Opposite, above: Market Street Craven Arms, *c.* 1900. The building on the right at the bottom of the street with the open arcade is the market hall, which was built in about 1888. The chapel on the right was erected in 1880 for the Primitive Methodists and opened on 29 June. To the right is London House, where James Overton began as a fishmonger in 1888. His daughter Jane married J.P. Wood, who later went on to form 'Chukie Chickens' with his three sons. The sons later bought the chapel and gave it to the Catholic Church as a memorial to their parents.

Opposite, below: The Shrewsbury Co-operative Society Ltd. Craven Arms, 1912. The shop stood on the corner of Dale Street and Newton Street and was there from about 1910. The shop faced strong opposition from Gaius Smith of Ludlow who had two shops in the town, one in Market Street and another in Corvedale Road. Other grocery shops in the town included Fredrick Miller, Henry Munn and Percy Proctor who were in Market Street, Sarah Gough whose business was in Station Road, Samuel Valentine whose premises were in Corvedale Road, and Annie Jukes who had shops in Market Street and Dale Road.

Station Road, Craven Arms, *c.* 1900. This is the main A49 road, looking towards Shrewsbury. The building on the left is the Temperance Hotel, built in 1865, which stands on the junction of the road leading to the railway station. It was described in 1885 as a 'family and commercial and family temperance hotel adjoining the Railway Station; good accommodation for commercial gentlemen, every comfort for tourists, good fishing, horses and traps for hire, terms moderate'. The house beyond is now the Fairview Bed and Breakfast. The garage on the right has been rebuilt but now stands empty, and the Craven Arms Evangelical Church now occupies the open space above.

Corvedale Road, Craven Arms, *c.* 1905. Corvedale Road is on part of the road leading to Wenlock. On a ground plan dated March 1881 four buildings are already marked, along with thirty-eight future building plots. Fryer Freeman's Fish Bar and the Spar Shop now occupy the building on the right. The building with the two gables is now Dale Street Personnel Ltd, Recruiting Services, and two houses to the left is J.K. Lunt the chemist. The open area in the foreground has now been built on, one of the buildings being the Wesleyan church, which was erected in 1913.

Newton Street, Craven Arms, c. 1910. Stokesay Castle Hotel is on the right with Stokesay School at the rear. The first national school was built near the church at Stokesay in 1858 and was enlarged in 1886 to accommodate 162 children. With the rapid growth of the town and a series of critical reports by inspectors, it was decided to build a new school near the centre of town. It opened on 31 August 1896 and cost between £2,000 and £3,000. The headmaster, Mr Thomas Mountford, transferred with the children and remained in the post until he retired in 1925.

Stokesay Castle Hotel, Craven Arms, c. 1960. The hotel was established in 1898 on Allcroft land and was run by Richard Hartshorn. The licence was transferred from the old Red Lion at Newton. By the 1930s the hotel was described as a family and commercial hotel run by a Mrs Helen Boulton. She advertised the following amenities. 'Tea Gardens, First Class Tariff, Excellent Cuisine, Separate Tables, Electric Lighting, Every Comfort, Home From Home, Fishing, Hunting, Golfing, Garage Adjoining, Cars For Hire, Tariff On Application.'

Stokesay Castle Hotel, 14 November 1968. The Craven Arms and District Chamber of Trade held a beer and sherry party and a ploughman's supper at the hotel. Having his glass filled by waiter David Scott is Harry Thompson the secretary of the chamber: on the right is Basil Wood, the president. In February 1966 the chef at the hotel was particularly proud of his Rainbow Trout Meunière, which was delicately browned and appetising and ready in less than two minutes.

Opposite, above: Wistanstow, *c.* 1905. This was an Anglo-Saxon settlement, sited on an ancient crossroads. It takes its name from St Wystan, a devout Christian prince, who declined the crown of Mercia. His uncle murdered him in AD 849. The school on the right was erected in 1859 to cater for 150 children. In latter years a dreadful extension has been built on the side, and in a recent publication the designer was branded 'an architectural hooligan'.

Opposite, below: The Grove, Craven Arms, *c.* 1920. At the beginning of the twentieth century this Victorian mansion was occupied by David Henry Greene QC. His widow continued to live there up until the Second World War, when it was commandeered by the military. In 1949 the estate was sold and five years later the mansion was demolished. J.P. Wood and Sons bought the estate in 1956 and over the next forty years a thriving poultry business was developed. At its height it employed around 1,500 people and processed up to 500,000 chickens a week under the brand name 'Chukie Chickens'. In 1968 the business was sold to Unilever, who in turn sold it to Unigate. The firm closed in the early 1990s.

Onibury, 21 December 1966. Although the history of Onibury goes back for centuries, this was the village's first official public house – opened just in time for Christmas. It was called the Holly Bush and was owned by Mr and Mrs John Briscoe. Maj. H. Holden had the privilege of pulling the first pint. The pub closed in about 1992 and is now the Ilex Studio. Ilex is the Latin name for holly.

Culmington Manor, *c.* 1920. The house stands on high ground, about 500 ft above sea level, and has a commanding view of the Corvedale. It's a fairly modern brick building erected in 1850 by Edward Wood. At the outbreak of the Boer War his son Gordon, a captain in the Shropshire Yeomanry, volunteered for service and was given command of the Thirteenth Company. They were soon engaging the enemy and fought battles at Linley, Heilbron, Kroonstad and Venderstroom. On 20 October 1900 while leading his men in battle outside Zeerust, Gordon was struck down, and while being carried on a stretcher received further wounds that killed him.

Hopesay Church and Rectory, *c.* 1930. St Mary's Church dates mainly from the thirteenth century. The tower built in about 1200 is squat and defensive with a similar pyramid roof as Clun Church. In the fifteenth century the nave was given a beautiful panelled roof of Spanish chestnut. The old stone rectory stands adjacent to the church.

Stokesay Court, *c.* 1920. This building was designed in the Tudor style by Thomas Harris and built for J.D. Allcroft in 1889. It has around 12 acres of land, parts of which are covered in banks of rhododendrons. H.J. Allcroft was a prolific traveller and collector. At the end of each journey he would have crates of souvenirs sent back from all over the world. During the Second World War, when the house was occupied by the military, they were boxed up, stored in the attic and forgotten. When the Allcrofts sold the house in 1994 the treasures were rediscovered, and a four day sale was held by Sotheby's, attracting buyers from all over the world.

Stokesay Castle, *c.* 1920. The de Say family were the Norman tenants of the manor, and shortly after 1068 Picot de Say built a castle and church on this site. Lawrence de Ludlow, a wealthy wool merchant, built the fortified manor house in about 1280. During the Civil War the church of St John the Baptist on the left was badly damaged by the Roundheads and was restored between 1654 and 1664, resulting in a rare Commonwealth church.

Stokesay Castle, *c.* 1920. The hall has been left practically unchanged. The staircase leads to the north tower, that the oldest part of the building and contains a well. The south tower, which can only be approached from the outside, leads to the solar, the private apartment of the lord. This contains an unusual carved fireplace and two peep holes that look down directly into the main hall.

The Revd E.H. Gilchrist De Castro, Vicar of Stokesay, 1908. The vicar sent out this portrait of himself on a calendar to his parishioners, for Christmas 1908, with the following message. 'My dear people, I am asked by so many for my portrait that I have at length decided to obtain one of the art blocks supplied by that indispensable firm the House of Home Words, so that all that receive this almanac will have their Vicar's watchful eye literally over them in 1909. May you also keep a good lookout on your vicar in turn and by your enthusiastic co-operation and constant attendance at worship, sustain him in the work of the Lord.'

Diddlebury, 14 July 1960. The village is known locally as Delbury and can trace its roots back to Saxon times. The Church of St. Peter has Saxon herringbone masonry. The ford is known as the Diddlebury Dip and the man on the tractor is Brian Corfield, a local farmer. His father Sydney and their dog Trudi are crossing the bridge. The family farmed at Church Farm, the white house near the church. It's believed the van belonged to Mr Price, the local butcher.

Delbury Hall, Diddlebury, *c.* 1930. The hall takes its name from what the locals call the village. It is a large plain brick building erected shortly after 1752. The staircase is a nice example of the period, with three slender twisted balusters to each tread. The grounds of the hall are now a trout fishery.

Munslow, *c.* 1955. The village lies on the main road from Craven Arms and many of the houses are built of Wenlock limestone. The cottages on the left have been carefully renovated; (*see* page 56). The Church of St Michael is a mixture of architectural styles, but dates back to Norman times. Inside, there is a large stone from the Great Wall of China, brought home by a naval relative of the vicar in 1884; it is used as a doorstop. A family by the name of Powell held the living there from 1776 until 1965.

Munslow, 24 August 1973. Members of Corvedale Royal British Legion clean up the war memorial that stands outside the Public Elementary (Endowed) School. The school was formerly the manor house of the Lyttleton family, and was endowed with £8 12s per annum, derived from money left and rent from land called the Parish Playground. On the memorial there are nine names from the First World War and three from the Second.

Munslow, *c.* 1910. The Corvedale winds its way through the village. The Crown Inn was once the Hundred House, a place where justice was dispensed in medieval times. Close by the war memorial on the left is a gabled stone house where Edward Littleton was born in 1589. He rose to become Chief Justice of north Wales and Solicitor General of England. He was also famous for changing sides in the run up to the English Civil War.

Corvedale School, 12 June 1981. After the sudden death of Mr Mitchell, the last headmaster of Diddlebury, the children were sent to Culmington School while Diddlebury was extended to form the new Corvedale School. When the new school was ready the schools at Culmington, Munslow and Stanton Lacy closed and the children moved to the new premises. The new headmaster was Richard Bray, who was appointed in January 1982. He opened the school to the children in February.

4

Cleobury Mortimer &
All Around the
Crooked Steeple

The crooked steeple, Cleobury Mortimer, 2 August 1973. St Mary's Church is the central and dominant point of the town. The main body of the church is early English in style, but its tower is Norman. The tall wooden steeple covered in oak shingles is warped by age and weather, giving it an unusual crooked look. In the Victorian east window is a memorial to the poet William Langland, the author of Piers Ploughman, who is reputed to have been born in Cleobury.

The High Street, Cleobury Mortimer, *c.* 1900. The Talbot has been an inn since about 1800. At the start of the twentieth century it belonged to Bridgnorth Brewery. The accommodation included an entrance hall, clubroom, bar, market room, sitting room, smoke room, commercial room and nine bedrooms; there was also stabling for twenty-one horses. The timber frontage is Victorian, built in about 1871 to mask a much older structure. The trees were planted to commemorate Queen Victoria's Diamond Jubilee in 1897.

The High Street, Cleobury Mortimer, *c.* 1905. Cleobury Mortimer is a small, charming, country town, sitting along the main road from Ludlow to Bewdley. The High Street has always been the centre of trade. In 1921 there were three grocers, two butchers, two drapers and clothiers, a coal merchant, a watchmaker and jeweller, a hardware store, a saddle maker, a tearoom and four boot shops.

The High Street, Cleobury Mortimer, 24 October 1962. Mrs Edith Harris, who had lived in the town for forty years, enjoying some late autumn sunshine. She is sitting by the stump of the old stone cross, said to mark the spot where Hugh de Mortimer erected a gallows in the thirteenth century and where the body of Prince Arthur was laid in 1502, on its journey from Ludlow to Worcester. The monumental horse trough and drinking fountain is a memorial to Captain Trow, who died of fever in South Africa during the Boer War.

Bridge explosion, Cleobury Mortimer, 9 March 1969. The operation to blow up the railway bridge that took the line from Cleobury Mortimer to Ditton Priors was known as 'Operation Cleoblow'. It took 80 lb of explosives and two controlled blasts to reduce the bridge to 200 tons of rubble. Army reservists from the Royal Monmouthshire Engineers carried out the work, half of whom were south Wales miners. Locals were keen to inspect the damage as they believed that a horde of gold sovereigns had been hidden by a bricklayer building the bridge and sealed in. As far as is known nothing was ever found.

Opposite, above: Lower Street, Cleobury Mortimer, *c.* 1935. The Wells, formally the town's main water supply lies to the right of the photograph. The cupola on the roof of the central building is over the Oddfellows Hall. The weather vane is shaped like a bricklayer's hod. At the beginning of the twentieth century the hall was much in demand for public concerts, which raised money for such good causes as supporting sufferers of smallpox and for improving the school premises.

Opposite, below: Cleobury Mortimer firemen, 10 August 1979. At the beginning of the twentieth century the town had a small fire station at the rear of the Market Hall and was manned by Captain Steven Conniff and eight men. To summon the men in 1932, an electric buzzer was fitted on the Market Hall, which could be heard half a mile away. In 1938 Ludlow Rural District Council took control of the brigade and bought them a new appliance before selling off their old equipment. The firemen moved to a new station in Lower Street in 1959. Back row, left to right: Sub. Officer John Davies, Ivor Booton, Leading Fireman Leslie Woodhouse, -?-. Front row: Jeff Shaw, Leading Fireman Robert Phillips, Tony Mullard.

Clee Hill, *c.* 1930. The road over Clee Hill is the main highway from Ludlow to Cleobury Mortimer. Titterstone Clee stands 1,749 ft above sea level and gives views of Herefordshire, Worcestershire, Gloucestershire and Staffordshire on a fine day. Many small settlements perched on the slopes can be cut off for days during hard winters. Following the blizzards of 1947, snow was piled higher than telegraph poles and people were seen standing on the roofs of their homes, trying to dig them out.

The Clee Hill Granite Co. quarry, *c.* 1870. Quarrying for the famous Dolerite or Dhu-stone started in about 1860, when about 2,000 people were employed. The stone was ideal for roadmaking as it set well under the roller, did not form sharp edges, made little dust, had good drainage and dried quickly. The Dhu-stone could also be broken into blocks and used for paving setts, kerbstones and gateposts. The chippings were good for making concrete, artificial stone and garden paths.

Abdon Clee stone quarry, *c.* 1910. Brown Clee stands just under 1,800 ft above sea level and is the highest point in Shropshire. One of the summits, Abdon Burf, once stood several feet higher but has been reduced over the years by quarrying for Dhu-stone. An incline railway, just over a mile in length, took the stone from the summit down to Ditton Priors.

Aerial ropeway, Clee Hill, *c.* 1920. During the early years of the last century a great many roads were upgraded for motor cars. Dhu-stone was in great demand and in 1909 a new quarry was opened at Magpie Hill by Thomas Roberts of Ludlow. The stone was moved off the hill to Detton Ford sidings by this aerial ropeway, erected by J.M. Henderson of Aberdeen.

The Radar Centre, Titterstone Clee, 12 September 1978. The summit of the hill has been used for many things in the past. Far back in history its flat peak was a fort. Mining for coal, limestone and Dhu-stone has taken place there and animals have always grazed its slopes. In recent times the Civil Aviation Authority's National Air Traffic Services have installed their radar at the top to track and guide aircraft. The large dome radar, which was opened on this date, gathers information on the weather.

The Crown, Knowbury, *c.* 1930. Knowbury is a fairly scattered village lying on the slopes of the Clee Hill slightly south of the main Ludlow to Cleobury Mortimer Road. The Crown was first granted a licence in about 1783. The inn was owned and managed by John Bowen in 1901 and the accommodation included two kitchens, two parlours, clubroom, five bedrooms and stabling for eight horses. Its main custom came from quarrymen, agricultural labourers and passing trade. It was sold in 1968 and is now a private house.

Stoke St Milborough, *c.* 1925. The village lies to the south-west of the Brown Clee and is huddled around its massive grey towered church. The name Stoke signifies a habitation while the second half of the name is derived from St Milburga, who founded Wenlock Priory. She was a great-granddaughter of the Mercian king, Penda. This is just one of only four churches dedicated to her in Britain.

The new Three Forked Pole, Corley Waste, 10 July 1972. Mr Priest, the parish clerk of Corley, stands in the bucket of a JCB to take away the chain and let the new three-forked pole stand free. It replaced the old pole, which had occupied that site for over 300 years and marks the spot where the three parishes of Corley, Bitterley and Hopton Wafers meet. Despite thick mist and pouring rain an enthusiastic crowd of over a hundred people attended the ceremony.

Bitterley Court, *c.* 1920. The house stands next to the church about half a mile east of the present village. The old settlement was moved in the sixteenth century to give the owners of the mansion a clear view. The court is mainly Jacobean with a Georgian front and was once the home of the Walcott family. The village used to be called Buterlie, the place where butter was made. Others believe its name stems from the cold weather in winter, giving rise to this old couplet. 'Bitterley, Bitterley under the Clee, Devil take me if I ever come to thee!'

The Gate Hangs Well, Farlow Common, *c.* 1970. The owner and licensee, Mr Randle Wallworth, rebuilt the pub in 1970. The architect was Aubrey H. Roper. The old inn dated from about 1830 and was owned by Admiral R. Woodward of Hopton Court. It consisted of a bar, tap room, parlour and four bedrooms. The landlord George Merrick was twice taken to court for allowing drunkenness on his premises. The first case in May 1892 was withdrawn on payment of costs and the second, two years later, was dismissed.

Farlow post office, 25 February 1974. The name of the village is derived from Fern Hill, on which the Church of St Giles, the school and a cluster of houses stand. The rest of the village, including the post office, lie at the foot of the hill down a steep winding lane. Until October 1844 Farlow was situated in Herefordshire. The first post office appeared in the village in about 1890, when Mrs Elizabeth Anslow was postmistress and the post office was situated at her husband's forge. Only letters were dealt with, post arriving at 10 a.m. and being dispatched at 4.20 p.m. on weekdays only. Cleobury Mortimer was still the nearest money order and telegraph office. To the left is Mrs Beddoes, who ran the post office in 1974.

Cleobury Court, Cleobury North, *c.* 1925. For many years this mansion was the home of the Hamilton Russell family. The Hon. C.E. Hamilton Russell was master of the Wheatland Foxhounds at the turn of the nineteenth century. A witch by the name of Prissy Morris once lived in the village. With just a look, it was said, she was able to stop a horse dead in its tracks.

Cleobury North watermill, 17 May 1939. The corn mill, which is mentioned in Domesday, is worked by water from the Cleobury brook, which rises in the village and is a tributary of the Rea. The iron water wheel was manufactured by John Hazledine of Bridgnorth. The mill has a unique and practical toilet, a small building running over the stream! The man in the photograph is William Green, who occupied the mill at this time.

The Crown Inn, Hopton Wafers, *c.* 1930. The village lies 2½ miles west of Cleobury Mortimer. The Crown was another inn owned by Admiral Woodward of Hopton Court. In 1901 it had a bar, a taproom, parlour, dining room, five bedrooms and stabling for three horses. The manager was Samuel Whitehead, who ran a good house and kept it clean and in good repair.

The Railway Inn, Neen Sollars, 9 November 1964. At this time the tavern was a Mecca for Midlanders, who would travel for miles for one of their duck suppers. By this time visitors would not have arrived by rail as passenger traffic had ceased in 1961 and goods traffic ended two years later in 1963. The inn was granted its first licence in about 1865.

Kinlet Hall, *c.* 1930. The hall was designed by Francis Smith of Warwick and built for the Childe family, the local lords of the manor. It dates from the first quarter of the eighteenth century. A large park was also laid out at this time: the family thought that the village spoilt their view, so they had it demolished and rebuilt on its present site. The village inn, the Eagle and Serpent, takes its unusual name from the Childe family's coat of arms.

An earlier house on the site belonged to the Blounts, a long-standing Shropshire family. Elizabeth Blount, one of Henry VIII's many mistresses, was the mother of the king's only acknowledged illegitimate child, Henry Fitzroy, Duke of Richmond and Somerset, thought by many contemporaries to be named as the heir to the throne over his two legitimate sisters: Mary and Elizabeth. Unfortunately, he died in 1536, the year before the birth of Prince Edward.

Opposite, above: Ditton Priors station, *c.* 1930. Plans were approved for the Cleobury Mortimer and Ditton Priors Light Railway in 1901, but work didn't begin on the project until 1907, with the line opening the following year. There were two stops, at Burwarton and Stotteston, with sidings at Aston Botterell, Prescott, Chilton and at Detton Ford when in 1909 an aerial ropeway was erected to carry stone from Tittestone Clee. In 1922 the line became part of the GWR. Passenger traffic ceased in 1938, and the line was taken over by the navy who opened an arsenal in the village. It is reported that the trains ran so slowly, because of their explosive loads, that the crews had enough time to jump off the footplate and set snares on the outward journey and on their return collect their catch.

Opposite, below: Ditton Priors, 19 January 1967. The depot at Ditton Priors was taken over by the United States military as a storage site on 10 January. This is the main entrance to the depot. The men are an advance party of American troops getting the camp shipshape before the arrival of 250 soldiers who were arriving two days later. During their stay several open days were held there, so that the locals could meet the men and sample a taste of American life.

St John the Baptist's Church, Kinlet, *c.* 1910. It is also said that the Childe family were not very impressed with the church, but instead of demolishing it they hid it behind a screen of trees so that all that can be seen is the tower peeping over the tops. The church has a Norman nave and chancel and transepts dating from the fourteenth century. It also contains a number of fine monuments to the Childe, Blount and Baldwin families. The nave is decorated for the harvest festival.

Kinlet Vicarage, *c.* 1920. In 1871 the living was in the gift of William Lacon Childe, the lord of the manor. The living included the vicarage and was valued at £360 plus 45 acres of glebe land. In 1871 the vicar was the Revd Edward George Childe-Baldwyn, a relation of the benefactor. He was also Honorary Chaplain to the Earl of Bradford and was made a Prebendary of Worham in Hereford cathedral. He was vicar of Kinlet for forty-four years, from 1846 until 1890.

5

To Ludlow & Beyond

Ludlow Castle and chapel, *c.* 1920. The chapel of St Mary Magdalene is Romanesque in style and was built between 1080 and 1120. Arthur, Prince of Wales and Katherine of Aragon were resident at Ludlow Castle until his untimely death there in 1502. Princess Mary had her household there and Henry Fitzroy was a Marcher Lord.

Sir Philip Sidney altered the castle between 1560 and 1586 to be used by the members of the Council of The Marches when they were in residence. The famous Elizabethan poet, Thomas Churchyard, described it as 'so bravely wrought, so fayre and fram'd, that to world's beauty may endure.'

The Feathers Hotel, Ludlow, *c.* 1905. The Feathers stands in the Bull Ring and was erected in about 1603. Its timber frame is elaborately carved and beautifully preserved. The inside of the building also contains many original features. Some of the fireplaces are said to have been taken from the castle. In earlier years the house was connected to the Council of The Marches, but has been an inn since at least 1656. To the right is Robert Crundell's shop. In 1891 he advertised as a gas power printer and bookbinder. He also sold commercial and fancy stationery, books, newspapers, magazines, framed prints and photographs.

Lower Broad Street, Ludlow, *c.* 1900. This area of town was where the poorer people involved in Ludlow's busy cloth industry lived. At the top is the Broad Gate, the last of the five main gateways in the town. The two semi-circular towers of stone are late medieval but the portcullis grooves and gate hinges are from the fourteenth century. The Wheatsheaf, to the right of the gate, was first recorded in 1753, and is the last of nine public houses that once existed in this part of Ludlow. It's also reputed to be the last hostelry in the town to brew its own beer.

The Butter Cross, Ludlow, *c.* 1935. The Butter or Market Cross, as it is sometimes known, was erected by the Corporation in 1743 on the site of the New House, an old timber-framed building. It cost in the region of £1,000 and was the work of architect William Baker of Audlem. The open ground floor was used for the sale of butter and other farm produce. In 1785 the Blue Coat Charity School reopened in the upper room of the Butter Cross with forty-five pupils on the roll. By the end of the nineteenth century a well-attended Workingmen's Evening Club was held there under the caring eye of the Revd E. Clayton and other clergymen.

The Rose and Crown, Ludlow, 21 April 1960. Two gentlemen sit in bright sunshine outside the inn enjoying a refreshing glass of beer. The tavern stands in Church Street and was first licensed in 1603 or 1604. In 1901 it was owned by Walter Thomas of Old Street Ludlow and managed by Walter Woodhouse. Ind, Coop and Co. leased the inn for a ten-year period in 1897, and it was only able to sell their ale during that time. In the past the inn was known for a short time as the Hole-in-the-Wall.

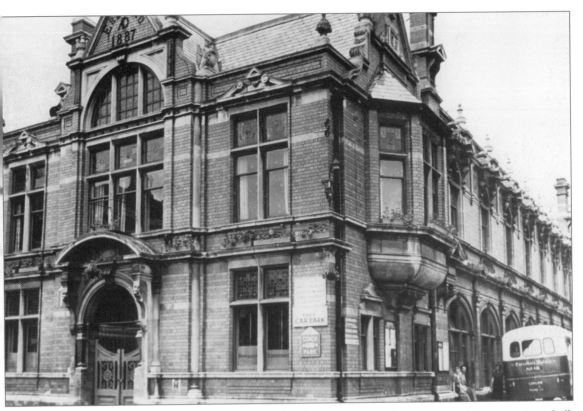

Ludlow Town Hall, 16 April 1958. At first the people of Ludlow were tremendously proud of their new town hall, which had replaced an earlier building erected in 1702. The Victorian hall cost about £6,000 and was described in *Kelly's Directory* of 1891 as 'a handsome building of red brick and Bath stone dressing, in the Renaissance style'. The architect was Henry A. Cheers of Twickenham, and the building comprised a market hall, assembly room, council chamber, retiring rooms, several offices and toilets. By the end of its life it was making such headlines in the local papers as 'Eyesore built in 1887' and 'Loyal citizens avert their eyes'.

Opposite, above: Broad Street, Ludlow, *c.* 1935. This street, with its elegant rows of Georgian and timber-framed buildings, has been described as 'one of the most memorable streets in England.' The Angel Hotel, with its two eighteenth-century bay windows, has been an inn since about 1555 and was used for coaching until the arrival of the railway. Lord Nelson addressed a cheering crowd from one of the windows, while staying there with his mistress Emma and her husband Sir William Hamilton in 1802. Napoleon's brother Lucien Bonaparte is reputed to have dined there, while a prisoner of war in the town in 1814.

Opposite, below: Castle Square, Ludlow, *c.* 1935. On the corner of Mill Street and the Square is Castle Lodge. The site, described by criminals sentenced by the Council of The Marches as 'a hell', was a prison in the early part of the sixteenth century. The lower section of the house was built in about 1564 for Thomas Sackford, an official of the Council of The Marches. The walls were once covered by plaster, which was removed by Thomas Roberts JP in 1895. The eighteenth-century town house on the right is now part of Ludlow College.

Ludlow Town Hall, *c.* 1925. The children and teachers of local Sunday Schools are gathered in the Assembly Room for an unknown event. In an 1895 guide the interior was described in this way: 'The large Hall is of grand proportions, the same size as the market space below, and lighted by large windows at the sides, and ornamental counter lights in the panelled ceiling. The walls are relieved by the arched windows, with frieze and dado in Lincrusta-Walton, and the platform at the end is flanked by coupled Scagliola marble columns on either side with classical capitals. The Council Chamber is a well proportioned and lofty room, thirty-four feet by twenty-five feet, and having its own separate entrance, and a handsome stone staircase approach from the north side of the building.'

Shrove Tuesday, Ludlow, 27 February 1968. This pancake race was the first public event to be held in the town since the restrictions laid down at the outbreak of the major foot and mouth epidemic the previous autumn. The event was organised by the Ludlow Ladies' Circle in aid of the Shropshire Voluntary Helping Hands Association. The event attracted over fifty competitors from as far afield as Brierley Hill. The Mayor, Mr W.J. Price, started the races. Prizewinners were Maureen Murry, Richard Ewels, Alan Woozencroft and Margaret Cooper, all from Ludlow Grammar School, Mrs Delia Kemp of Ludlow and Mrs Joan Reed, chairman of Bridgnorth Ladies' Circle.

Ludlow Town Hall, 17 March 1986. This photograph was taken from the top of St Laurence's tower and shows the roof being removed from the town hall at the beginning of demolition. It was the end of a lovely piece of Victoriana, which by the last quarter of the twentieth century had gone out of fashion and was described in the Shropshire volume of Pevsner's 'Buildings of England' in this way: 'All these streets abut on to Ludlow's bad luck, the Market Hall of 1887 by Harry A. Cheers of Twickenham. There is nothing that could be said in favour of its fiery brick or useless Elizabethan detail.'

The horse and rider statue, Ludlow Town Hall, 19 March 1986. During the demolition a crane was used to remove this plaster-cast copy of a bronze Boer War memorial that stands in the centre of Adelaide in Australia. It shows an Australian soldier heading for battle on his horse. It is the work of Ludlow sculptor Capt Adrian Jones, who was born in 1845. He lived to the great age of ninety-three, becoming a very fashionable artist with his work being displayed all around the world.

Castle Street, Ludlow, *c.* 1900. The eastern end of Castle Street was known locally as Post Office Square from the post office at No. 6, run at this time by Postmaster William Price. On the left is the end of the old Town Hall and to the right is the end of The Rows. The building at the end of Church Street and Harp Lane housed the business of Fredrick Larcombe. In 1905 he was a cycle agent but also sold sewing machines, mangles, mail carts and musical instruments for cash or 'by easy payment system'.

Brown's chemist shop, Ludlow, *c.* 1905. William Brown traded as a pharmaceutical chemist from 49 Bull Ring. The firm was founded in the 1860s by Alfred Marston and taken over by Mr Brown in about 1900. In 1905 he was the manager of the Shropshire Horse and Cattle Food Co. He was also the manufacturer of Marston's Celebrated Corn Eradicator, which sold at 9*d* or 1*s* 1*d* a bottle, post-free.

Smith's Supply Store, Ludlow, *c.* 1900. The Supply Stores were founded over a hundred years before as Harding's Tea Warehouse. The purity and excellence of their teas were the key to their success, and the head of the business, Mr Gaius Smith, kept in direct commercial touch with a leading firm of tea importers. As well as tea dealers they were also bacon curers, coffee roasters, tallow chandlers, general grocers and patent medicine vendors. They also had shops at the Sandpits in Ludlow, Craven Arms, Much Wenlock and North Malvern. Mr Smith was Mayor of Ludlow in 1898.

The Clifton Cinema, Old Street, Ludlow, 2 April 1987. Alfred Temple, a travelling showman, opened Ludlow's first cinema in the Assembly Rooms in 1909. The Clifton was a purpose-built cinema, which opened in 1938 on the site of Noakes' Yard and Dean's Yard. In the 1970s, with the rapid decline of the film industry, the cinema was converted into a bingo hall. After a great deal of argument it was demolished, and a sheltered housing complex named Clifton Court now occupies the site.

Ludlow Cottage Hospital, *c.* 1960. The hospital was in College Street, and was opened in 1874 in a building once used by the Palmer's Guild. It was established 'for the relief of the labouring classes, towns folk only being admitted free'. It was endowed by the Hon. Mary Windsor-Clive who died in 1889. In 1937 it had eleven beds for patients. This photograph shows the hospital being closed for six weeks while work on fire precautions takes place. The hospital staff are, left to right: Sister Marjorie Matthews, Matron O.M. Laycock, Auxiliary Nurse Madge Webb, Staff Nurse Sheila Morris, SEN Bertha Nason. The hospital finally closed in 1982.

Derailment at Ludlow, 1 February 1961. 'In a cloud of hissing steam and smoke the engine hurtled into one end of the concrete platform, tore up several yards of it and then ground to a halt, tilting almost on its side.' This was the dramatic way in which a local newspaper described the accident. The goods train had left Shrewsbury with twenty wagons, taking them to Pontypool Road via Hereford. At Ludlow the driver was shunting his train when the engine ploughed through a stop block and crashed into the platform. The drive, J. Layton, and the fireman, D.A. Carter, managed to jump to safety and the guard, D. Barr, also escaped uninjured. After the crash single line traffic had to be enforced through the station. The signal box was also badly affected, with all the signals having to be operated manually. The engine was a Class 5 nicknamed 'Black 5'.

Dinham Bridge, Ludlow, *c.* 1935. The bridge is overlooked by the impressive ruins of Ludlow Castle. It has three arches and there are half columns above the watercuts. It dates from around 1825, and replaced a wooden bridge built on stone piers. One of the paths near the bridge is known as Bread Walk.

St Laurence's Church, Ludlow, *c.* 1925. This magnificent parish church was rebuilt on a grand scale between 1433 and 1471. The choir and chancel are around 80 ft long and at the east end is the beautiful window, telling the story of St Laurence, the patron saint of the church. It was painstakingly restored by David Evans of Shrewsbury who completed it in 1832. The stalls are fine examples of fifteenth-century woodwork and the misericords, depicting life in medieval England, are reputed to be one of the finest series in the country.

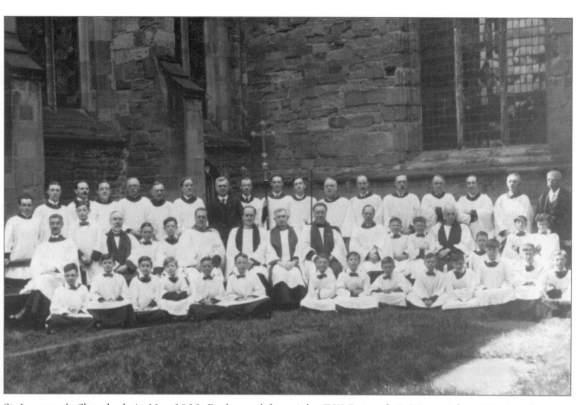

St. Laurence's Church choir, May 1923. Back row, left to right: T.W. Barnard, E. Wainwright, W. Price, T.J. Evans, W.C. Tyrell, R.J. Thomas, E.W. Lethbridge, T.H. Higgins (Churchwarden), C.T. Evans, P. Barker, W. Holt, S.H. Valentin (Churchwarden), H. Price, J.R. Evans, W. Parsonage, R. Ridgley, W.J. Brown, R.B. Brookes (Vestry Clerk and Verger). Middle row: J. Diggle, G. Richards, Ven. Arch Deacon Maude, C.C. Meredith, F.E. Bastick (Organist and Choirmaster), Revd W.F. Taylor (Reader), Revd A.E.Ll. Kenyon (Rector), Revd S. Bailey (Preacher), J.H. Lockhart (Sacristan), G. Harris, D. Watkins, Revd J. Mackay, A.R. Badlan, C. Meredith, J. Baker. Front row: L. Backer, T. Davies, T. Went, J. Richards, W. Cadwallader, A. Davies, W. Pratt, G. Rickards, R. Stephens, G. Jones, A. Jackson, J. Richards, W. Holt, F. Pratt. Mr Bastick was organist and choirmaster from 1917 until 1948.

Milton's Masque of *Comus*, Ludlow Castle, July 1934. This epic restaging of Milton's classic marked the 300th anniversary of its premier, performed to mark the first visit of the Lord President of The Marches, the Earl of Bridgwater. The play was performed again in 1953, 1958 and 1959 as a fundraising exercise for St Laurence's Church. Its success led to the foundation of the first Ludlow Festival in 1960. This is a scene from Episode Three, the Trial of Prince David of Wales at Shrewsbury, 30 September 1283. Acting in this scene are Lady Berwick, Lady Anne Bridgeman and Lady Joan Bridgeman.

Mrs Edgerton Hine, Ludlow Castle, July 1934. Mrs Edgerton Hine was very involved in amateur dramatics in Shropshire and was chosen as stage manager for Episode Three. Each episode seems to have been organised individually, with its own chairman and committee. Shrewsbury's Mayor, Mr Richard Mansell, was chairman of this group. Amateur dramatic groups still compete each year for the Edgerton Hine Cup, named in honour of Mrs Edgerton Hine.

Ludlow Festival, June 1984. Ludlow Festival goes from strength to strength each year and the jewel in the crown of the festival is always the open-air performance of one of Shakespeare's plays, against the amazing backdrop of the castle. The play performed during the 1984 season was *A Midsummer Nights Dream*, directed by Peter Cregeen. The actors are left to right, Peter MacKriel, Jim MacManus, Derek Smith, Michael Goldie, Robin Hayter, John Hartley with Willie the dog.

Ludford Mill and Horseshoe Weir, *c.* 1870. The Horseshoe Weir was designed to supply water to mills on either side of the River Teme. The mill on the Ludford side of the Teme was a fulling mill, built in medieval times to clean and beat cloth. It was given to the Palmers' Guild in about 1349. The right-hand section of the building has been demolished. At one time there were eight water mills on the Teme around Ludlow.

The Whitcliffe, Ludlow, *c.* 1900. The Whitcliffe takes its name from the white limestone that was quarried there and used to build so many of Ludlow's buildings. The area was used for grazing animals, and in the eighteenth century it became a fashionable place to promenade.

The Old Bell Inn, Ludford, c. 1890. Humphrey Powell (a member of the Council of The Marches) built this house in the early seventeenth century. It became an inn at an early date and was first known as the Three Crowns and then the Bell. In the eighteenth century it was a coaching house, but when the new road bypassed it in the 1820s it was converted into a pair of cottages. In 1910 the house was converted back to a single dwelling.

Ludford House and St Giles' Church, c. 1890. Ludford is a small settlement on the south bank of the River Teme. Part of the church dedicated to St Giles dates from the Norman period, while the chancel was altered in about 1300 and the Fox Chapel added in 1555. Ludford House is late Elizabethan or early Jacobean in style, though an earlier house stood on this site from at least the twelfth century.

Bromfield, *c.* 1910. Bromfield is a picturesque village, standing on the River Teme, north-west of Ludlow. Its name is derived from the golden broom that once flourished in the surrounding fields. The church is part of the old priory church. Inside there is a memorial to Dr Henry Hickman, the pioneer of anaesthetics. The building across the river is the sawmill, and the reciprocating saw used there has now been installed at the Blist Hill Open Air Museum.

The Gatehouse, Bromfield, 7 November 1954. The Gatehouse is another fragment of the old Benedictine Priory of St Mary that was suppressed by Henry VIII in about 1540. It was built of broad stone with a timber-framed upper storey and a gable that dates from the fourteenth century. In the past it has been used as a village school and as a reception room.

Bromfield post office, *c.* 1910. At the beginning of the twentieth century William Wadeley was sub-postmaster and to supplement his wage he was also the village tailor. Incoming mail reached the post office at 4.30 a.m. and outgoing mail left at 6 a.m. and 8.30 p.m. There is a meadow in Bromfield called The Crawls, which was once the site of a moated mansion. The owner had a beautiful daughter who fell in love with a penniless knight. This so angered the father that he swore the only dowry she would receive would be the land she could crawl around on a harsh winter's night. Wearing leather breeches, she amazed her father by crawling all the way to Downton. He was so impressed he made her his heiress over her brothers.

Downton Castle, *c.* 1910. This is not an ancient border castle as its name suggests, but was built in 1774 by Richard Payne Knight, MP for Ludlow. The Knights were ironfounders and had a wide variety of business interests, which included furnaces at Bouldon, Charlecotte and Brigewood. All three were supplied with iron ore from the Clee Hills. The Knights paid a great deal of attention to landscaping their gardens, and during the nineteenth century they introduced many exotic flowers, shrubs and trees to their estate.

The Hay water mill, Downton, *c.* 1900. This picturesque water mill on the banks of the Teme is said to belong to one of the forges that made nails. The forge used charcoal as fuel and the water wheel operated the bellows that provided the blast of air. The mill probably dates from the early seventeenth century. It fell into a bad state of repair and was demolished.

Ashford Carbonell, *c.* 1900. The name Ashford is derived from the ford and the great ash that stood by it; they are thought to have been situated a little further downstream than the present bridge. Carbonell was the family name of the lord of the manor, William Carbonell. The houses all straggle along the main street and are a mixture of architectural styles. The funeral cortège of Prince Arthur, eldest son of Henry VII, is believed to have used this route on its way back to London.

Ashford water mill, Ashford Carbonell, 7 July 1973. The water mill was originally used to grind corn but was later adapted as a sawmill. It has also been used to grind cattle feed, to generate electricity and to pump water to Ashford Court. In 1973 Richard's Castle School visited the mill as part of their school project. Mr A.G. Froggatt then owned it. Left to right: Alison Cole, Sarah Phillips, Peter Froggatt, Kim Shepherd, Tim Froggatt and Nigel Davies with the model water wheel.

Whitton and Greete School, *c.* 1926. Back row, left to right: Ivan Horton, Tom Hoskins, Jeff Jukes, Bob Davies, Reg Smith, Fred Turner, William Mapp, Charlie Wozencroft. Third row: Phyllis Thomas, Gladys Wozencroft, Elsie Davies, -?-, Sylvia Plevey, May?, Nancy Smith. Second row: -?-, Isabel Wozencroft, Rene Mackie, Edith Cartmell, Molly Jones, Evelyn Chapman, Nellie Breakwell, Marjorie Davies, Phyllis?, Front row: George Wozencroft, Bernard Wozencroft, Arnold Bounds, Bernard Bounds, David Wall, Reg Butcher. Elsie Davies recalls she won first prize at the West Midland Show for her needlework and received a book on the subject that was worth 7s 6d. She also won a bronze medal for an essay she wrote on Empire Day and once received a penny from an inspector for having the neatest books in the school.

The Salwey Arms, Wooferton, *c.* 1970. The inn has been fully licensed since 1853. In 1900 the owner was Mrs O'Brian of Moor Park, Ludlow, and the landlady was Elizabeth Gittins. This photograph was taken when it was discovered that the licensee, Mr Harold Moulton, and his sister Phyllis had been bound and gagged after a midnight raid. Mr Moulton was Shropshire's longest serving landlord at the time. The robbers got away with over £200.

6

The Quietest Under the Sun

Aston-on-Clun, *c.* 1910. The name Aston-on-Clun is derived from East-of-Clun, and the village was referred to as Eston in Domesday. It also has a public house called the Kangaroo Inn, reputed to be the only one of that name in the country. There is a forge garage, which was once the blacksmith's shop, and in a field at the rear of the village hall the foundations of a deserted settlement have been found.

Aston-on-Clun, 29 May 1937. Every year on Oak Apple Day the ceremony of dressing the Arbor Tree takes place. Locals believe that the flags commemorate the marriage of Mary Carter of Sibdon and John Marston of Aston-on-Clun, whose wedding took place on 29 May 1786. Historians trace its roots back to Celtic times, when women's clothing was hung on sacred trees in spring to ensure the fertility of the crops during the coming year.

Aston-on-Clun, 26 May 1986. This is the 200th anniversary celebrations when local schoolchildren re-enacted the marriage of Mary Carter and John Marston. The tradition of tree dressing was kept alive by the Marston family, who paid for the flags each year until the 1950s, when the responsibility was taken over by Hopesay Parish Council. The old tree was a Native or English Poplar, believed to be over 300 years old when it was blown down in a gale in 1995. A young tree has replaced it and the custom continues each year.

Clun, *c.* 1930. There has been human activity in this area for over 5,000 years. There was a Bronze Age settlement near the site and the Saxons had a thriving community here before the arrival of the Normans. The town prospered, and in the fourteenth century it received a royal charter to hold a weekly market and two annual fairs. The prosperity of the town declined in the nineteenth century because the railway passed it by.

Clun Castle and lake, *c.* 1930. Parts of the castle still remain, but the lake has disappeared. The lake was man-made and lined with clay. After the Second World War it was sold to a Birmingham businessman who, not knowing its history, tried to clean out the weed using a bulldozer; this disturbed the clay and the water ran out. The lake provided power for one of the water mills and was stocked with thousands of fish. The first castle was a motte-and-bailey construction, erected by Picot de Say and mentioned in Domesday. It was strategically placed and was in the first line of defence against attacks by the Welsh. The author Sir Walter Scott lodged for several months at the Buffalo Hotel in Clun, where he wrote his novel *The Betrothed*, basing his Garde Dloureuse on Clun Castle.

Market day, Clun, *c.* 1900. The excited children are standing outside the post office, run for many years by Jessie Cooke. Top left is the sign of the Buffalo Hotel and opposite is the wagon belonging to Rix's grocery store in the High Street. The white building in the centre is the North and South Wales Bank, who only opened on Tuesdays from 11 a.m. until 2 p.m. and on fair days; they were backed by the London Westminster Bank. Sherwood's butcher's shop is on the corner of the buildings on the right and next to them is the White Horse Inn, run for many years by Mrs Graves, who died in the early 1920s aged eighty-five. The wheel in front of the inn was used to wind drinking water up from the well. A poultry dealer sits on his crates of chickens, while a 'cricker', the local name for a travelling china salesman, sets out his wares on the pavement.

Opposite, above: High Street, Clun, *c.* 1930. The large house on the right is Creswell House in Bridge Street. The shop next door was a draper and outfitter run by T. and A. Hamar; the premises are now converted into two cottages known as Albany House and Alpha Cottage. On the left is the Malt House, built in 1619. By 1819 Richard Thomas was the maltster, but by 1841 the business had been taken over by George Hamar. At the beginning of the twentieth century it was an inn called the Old Talbot, run by Joe Luther. Today part of the Maltings has been converted into a pleasant little café.

Opposite, below: Clun Women's Institute, *c.* 1946. Clun WI was founded on 18 August 1931. By 1960 they met every second Tuesday of the month at the Church Room at 6.30 pm. The oldest WI in the area was Clungunford who were founded on 11 October 1922; Clunbury WI was started seven years later on 16 July 1929.

The lych-gate, Clun, *c.* 1920. The gate was erected in about 1723, has four gables and is built of wood with stone tiles. It has an interesting history. In 1839 it was sold to a local gentleman who had it as an arbour in his garden. A few years later the curate, the Revd E.C. Swainson, retrieved the gate, but the parishioners would not allow him to restore it to the original site as they preferred the more convenient access next to the Six Bells Inn. However, they allowed the curate to resite it at the west end of the churchyard to keep the cows away. In 1877 the gate was finally restored to its original site.

St George's Church, Clun, *c.* 1930. Parts of the church date from the Norman period, but the almost round site on which the church is built indicates it occupies a much older holy place. During the Civil War it was occupied by Roundheads, and was partly destroyed by fire in a Royalist attack. There was extensive restoration carried out in 1877 under the direction of G.E. Street. At this time the whole of the chancel was rebuilt; the ancient canopy there is thought to have been over a medieval altar. The church register dates back to 1653, but it is believed that an organist at the church, who was so shocked by what he read, destroyed an older one!

The Bell Procession, Clun, 22 July 1914. The bells had been recast in London and were returned by rail to Broome station. There they were met by two decorated drays, local clergymen, church officials, almsmen and a horde of excited children. They were then paraded back to Clun for the welcoming home of the bells ceremony. Here the parade is marching down Church Street, carrying banners with the legends 'God Bless The Bells', 'Pease Be Unto Clun 1668', and 'Welcome The Bells'. Hymns were sung by the lych-gate, and after an address from the vicar everyone paraded round to the vicarage for a refreshing tea and sports events. The building by the bridge is the Temperance Hall, erected in 1870, now converted into the Bridge Crafts and Coffee Shop.

Clun bells, 22 July 1914. From left to right: Revd Vaughan (from Newcastle), Mr W. Mead, Revd Harold Scott (resident chaplain to Holy Trinity Hospital), Mr G. Townsend, Revd R. Machen, Mr Darrell, Mr J. Davies, -?-, Revd Cope.

Clun Show, *c.* 1910. The show was held in the castle grounds where a variety of sports took place throughout the day. They consisted of horse leaping, pony races, athletics, children's races and tug-of-war. This last event was very popular and taken very seriously by teams of young labourers from the surrounding area. A special race for the ladies included washing clothes in a tub and running with them to a washing line to hang them out.

The maypole dray, Clun, *c.* 1910. In about 1900 the Clun Show became an annual event. A great favourite with the crowds was the maypole dray. At one time the dray was decorated the night before with wild flowers but in later years it was the young girls who wore the flowers in a garland around their hair. The dray and horse's harness was also plaited with flowers. The girls and the maypole would be paraded around the town to the castle grounds, where the pole would be set up on flat ground by the river and the girls would dance at intervals throughout the day.

Patriotic sale, Clun, 8 September 1915. During the First World War many fundraising events were held to raise money for the men fighting in the trenches. This event was held in a local farmyard and was opened by Lady Powis, which encouraged everyone to turn out in their best clothes. The legend between the patriotic posters reads, 'It's Our Flag, Fight For It, Work For It'.

Holy Trinity Hospital, Clun, c. 1935. Henry Howard, the Earl of Northampton, founded the Hospital in 1614. It housed twelve poor men, who were to live a life of piety and to pray for the soul of their benefactor. In return the almsmen received 10s a week, 3 tons of coal a year, a faggot of wood a month, clothing, a pint of milk and a pint of beer a day and a free dinner on Sundays and feast days, which were eaten in the hall.

Almsmen, Clun, 9 September 1935. Four members of Holy Trinity Hospital stand by the lych-gate outside St George's Church, dressed in their traditional uniform. This consisted of a hat and a dark blue coat with the coat-of-arms of the founder, a rampant silver lion on a red background. The formidable character in the centre is John Weale of Newcastle-on-Clun. He was known as 'Joe the Bear', a nickname he earned by wrestling bears at the May fair in Knighton. In later life he contented himself by sitting on a bench in the middle of Clun and tripping up girls and young ladies with his walking stick. There is a statue commemorating 'Joe the Bear' at the hospital. The two almsmen on the right are Mr Whittle and Mr Edwards.

St Cuthbert's Church, Clungunford, *c.* 1910. The name of the village is derived from Clun, the river, Gunnas, a Saxon lord, and ford, a river crossing. The oldest building in the village is the church, which dates from the Norman period. Standing by the church is the motte or mound of the old castle; both stand by the river while the village straggles up the hill. The first bridge to cross the river at this point was erected in 1657.

Clungunford School, *c.* 1910. The school was opened in 1855 as a public elementary mixed school. Built to take 128 children, the average attendance in 1905 was 92. There were only two teachers at this time, John Turner, the master, and Mrs Turner the sewing mistress. The school was under the control of Clun Local School Attendance Committee.

Clunton, *c.* 1910. According to the old rhyme, 'Clunton, Clunbury, Clungunford and Clun are the quietest places under the sun.' The sleepy little hamlet of Clunton lies on the River Clun, south of Bishop's Castle. During the nineteenth century it boasted a school, a post office, Methodist Church and public house, all except the Crown Inn have now closed. The church is dedicated to St Mary and was erected in 1871 as a chapel of ease to St Swithin's at Clunbury. A magnificent Iron Age fort stands on the top of Sunny Hill, north-west of the village.

The Clunbury Oddfellows' Procession, *c.* 1910. Friendly societies were very popular in South Shropshire at the beginning of the twentieth century. There were Oddfellow Lodges at Clunbury and Bishop's Castle and an Ancient Order of Forester Lodges at Aston-on-Clun, Clun, Craven Arms and Lydbury North. They were often involved in the organisation of local events, as well as parading around the local villages several times a year, calling on local dignitaries for food and refreshment. They dressed in their Sunday best and wore collars, sashes and bowler hats. They also carried large, colourful, silk embroidered banners at the head of their parade to signify which lodge they belonged to.

Norbury School, *c.* 1905. This public elementary school was built of Norbury and Bath stone. It cost £2,500 and was paid for by a Mrs Scott of Stourbridge, opening in September 1874. It was described in 1891 as 'an elegant feature on the plain, west of the Stretton Hills, where it is conspicuous from a long distance and is seen from the Craven Arms and Bishop's Castle line'.

Abcott Manor, Clungunford, *c.* 1930. The manor is a large Elizabethan half-timbered structure, with some curiously moulded brick chimney-stacks. It has some fine panelled rooms with plastered ceilings. The main beams are decorated with trailing branches of pomegranates and a series of five circular medallions each contain a different design, a stag, a lion, a unicorn, a goat and a horned beast. At the beginning of the twentieth century it was a farmhouse, and had been the home of the Prince family for several generations.

Bedstone Court, *c.* 1910. The mansion was built in the Elizabethan style in 1884 by the architect Thomas Harris, the author of *Victorian Architecture*. It was erected for Sir Henry Ripley MP; whose great-grandfather had made the family fortune by opening a dye works in Bradford. The house is a 'calendar house', having 365 windows, fifty-two rooms and twelve chimneys. Sir Henry left the Court in 1903 to live at Bedstone House. The mansion was then occupied by Mrs H.W. Langley, but has now been converted into a successful boarding school. After a recent fire the building has been beautifully restored.

St Mary's Church, Bedstone, *c.* 1910. The church owes its origin to the Normans. It has a nave, chancel and a timber-framed tower at the west end with a shingled spire. There is also a stained glass window in the north wall by William Kemp that dates from 1899. The church was completely restored in 1879 at a cost of £1,200. The work was carried out under the direction of a Mr Kempson, architect for Hereford Diocese.

Bucknell forge, *c.* 1900. Bucknell has always been a thriving little village. As well as the usual amenities there were also a thatcher, a cobbler, a coal merchant, a steam threshing machine proprietor, a wheelwright, a blacksmith and four public houses. At the end of the nineteenth century the smithy and one of the public houses, the Plough Inn, were run by the same man, John Dodd. In 1885 he advertised: 'One minute's walk from the Station, a good horse and trap for hire, good stabling, well-aired beds'.

Bucknell Show, *c.* 1920. The donkey cart belonged to Arthur Whittle on the left. His brother Stan is the man with the fiddle. Arthur was the village postman, who used the cart to supplement his wages by fetching coal and other goods from the station and delivering them around the village. The show flourished throughout the first half of the twentieth century.

Bucknell station, *c.* 1900. The line was opened in 1863 to take traffic from Shrewsbury into central Wales via Craven Arms and through to Swansea and Camarthen. The railway altered the life of the village, opening it up to most parts of the country. The elegant stone station on the right, which is now unmanned, is one of the finest on the line and has won prizes for its floral displays in summer. On the left are the small wooden waiting room, the signal box and the home starting signal. The goods yard is on the right behind the train.

Newcastle-on-Clun, *c.* 1925. The village is set in a scenic valley at the confluence of the River Clun and the Folly brook. The Church of St John the Baptist dates from early Victorian times and has an unusual revolving lych-gate. On a hillside immediately above the village is Fron Camp, an Iron Age hill fort.

7

To Bishop's Castle & Over the Stiperstones

St John the Baptist's church, Bishop's Castle, *c.* 1935. The church was built in 1291 and stands at the bottom of the town. The main body of the church was destroyed by fire during the Civil War, although the tower survived. The church was rebuilt in 1648 and heavily restored in 1860. There is a red line around the base of the tower that was used in a game called Fives. There are a number of interesting tombstones in the churchyard. One records the death of Lt Col Louis Pace of the French Light Cavalry, who died on 1 May 1814. There are also records of babies being fathered by French prisoners on parole! These men were allowed to walk out alone to a white post on either side of the town. The distance was remembered for many years as 'The Frenchman's Mile'.

Bishop's Castle from the church tower, *c.* 1930. Bishop's Castle was described by Sir Richard Colt Hoare in his diary in June 1799 in this way: 'I found a comfortable inn (the Castle). The Inn, its garden and the bowling green above it occupy the space of the Bishop's castle – here the bishop formerly resided-til about the time of Q. Elizabeth. The town is a borough – commanded by Lord Clive – dreary and dull – the ground around it is uncommonly rich and valuable – owing probably to the quantity of manure running down on it from the town on all sides. (Inn Good).'

Church Parade, Bishop's Castle, 20 March 1967. This is the last Church Parade by the Mayor and Corporation before they amalgamated with South Shropshire District Council. The Corporation consisted of a mayor, four aldermen and twelve councillors. The municipal insignia comprised two silver maces dated 1697, two silver-topped staves carried by the mayor and ex-mayor, a mayor's chain of office, a town crier's staff and a common seal. The maces can be seen at the rear of the parade. At the time of their amalgamation Bishop's Castle was believed to be the smallest borough in England. The town is also proud of the fact that it has retained the post of mayor in preference to a chairman.

Charter Celebrations, Bishop's Castle, 20 July 1973. This was the 400th anniversary of the charter granted by Queen Elizabeth I in 1573. By 1585 two members of parliament were being returned and the town was known as a 'rotten borough'. The elections were full of bribery and corruption, and it was alleged in 1722 that one MP had paid fifty-two of the fifty-three electors who had voted for him. In the 1820 election all four candidates were returned, as each had polled eighty-seven votes! The two men, Alan Davies and Rolly Higgins (right), are contestants in the Best Beard competition.

Bishop's Castle Tennis Club, c. 1910. The tennis club played on a court at Oak Meadow. Another club was founded by the Bishop's Castle WI, who built a court on land behind Hemming's garage. The distinguished gentleman with the white beard is Arthur Greenhous, a former mayor of the town. He ran a business in Market Square that was listed as a general and manufacturing ironmonger's. He kept a wide range of agricultural implements and dairy appliances in stock and a wide variety of seeds.

Greenhous buses, Bishop's Castle, *c.* 1910. At the beginning of the twentieth century Arthur Greenhous's son Vincent went into the family business. While working for his father he began to show an interest in the motor vehicles of the day and saw their tremendous possibilities for the future. He persuaded his father to open a garage in the town, negotiated the agency for Ford and ran a fleet of buses to Shrewsbury and around the local villages. Vincent branched out on his own in 1913 when he opened his first garage in Meadow Place in Shrewsbury.

Bishop's Castle, 16 June 1965. These schoolgirl-only toilets in Union Street were quite unique, as they are believed to be the only lavatories that discriminated between the ages of its users. Until their demolition they left many a poor visitor hopping around in a confused state!

The House on Crutches, Bishop's Castle, 20 March 1961. The house was built between 1610 and 1630 and experts believe it has hardly been altered since the seventeenth century. The two young schoolboys make their way up the one-in-three gradient cobbled path under the ancient house.

The House on Crutches, Bishop's Castle, 2 April 1986. The house takes its name from the supports under the upper storey. In 1986 the Old Castle Land Trust purchased the house and an appeal was launched for its restoration, which was sympathetically carried out by 1988. During the restoration a number of modern carvings were added. It is now a museum covering different areas of local life and is run by volunteers at weekends.

Bishop's Castle station, *c.* 1910. The line was opened in 1865 from Craven Arms to Bishop's Castle with a short junction to Lydham Heath. The overall plan was to extend the line to Montgomery and on to the Welsh coast, but the line never prospered and was closed in 1935 with no more track being laid. Other stations on the line were at Eaton, Plowden and Hordeley. In 1891 John Craston was manager of the line and Edward Phillips was stationmaster. There was a special bus service for passengers between the station and Castle Hotel.

Bishop's Castle Fire Brigade, *c.* 1915. In 1891 the fire station was in Welsh Street but the keys were kept at W.R. Robinson's in Union Street, George Strawson was captain of twenty men. By 1905 Mr Strawson was still in charge, but the number of firemen had dropped to six and the station had moved to Union Street. The new fire engine 'caused great admiration,' when it was bought. It was horse drawn and the horse had to be brought down from the Castle Hotel or caught in the field at the bottom of the town, which could cause a delay. The mayor is Mr E.C. Davies, a local ironmonger, Mr Lockley is wearing the bowler hat, and on the other side of the mayor is John Lewis, the captain of the brigade. Mr Emmanuel Beddoes, a local builder, is sitting on the right of the engine.

The Three Tuns, Salop Street, Bishop's Castle, *c.* 1910. Nearly thirty public houses have been identified in Bishop's Castle, but the most famous is the Three Tuns. It was bought quite by chance by John Roberts, a tea taster from London, in 1888 and it was run by the Roberts family for three generations until his grandson, also called John, retired in 1976. The first thing Mr Roberts did after buying the inn was build a new brewery. He also employed his cousin, who was teetotal, to brew the beer! Brewing is still carried out there today and the beer is always of the highest standard.

Welsh Street, Bishop's Castle, *c.* 1900. Egwin, a Saxon lord gave the town to the church after he had received a cure at the tomb of St Ethelbert in Hereford Cathedral. The town's name was then changed to Bishop's Castle. This view is looking towards Market Square.

Bishop's Castle Secondary School, *c.* 1930. The school opened in 1922 after a long battle with Clun over which town should have it. Bishop's Castle won but Walter Vaughn from Clun salvaged some pride back, as he was the first pupil to be registered at the school. Only eighty pupils turned up on the first day, a lot fewer than Mr C.W. Dobson, the first headmaster, expected but the reason for the poor attendance was put down to the wet weather. The buildings were clad with dangerous asbestos, but were not demolished until the 1980s.

Plowden Hall, *c.* 1910. The Hall is situated in a village of the same name, which is derived from the 'valley where the deer play' or the 'valley where sports are played'. It nestles among the hills and was built by Edmund Plowden in about 1557. Inside remains much of the old oak panelling and a fine Jacobean mantlepiece. Inside the chapel is an unusual brass representing Edmund's father Humphrey. The house is rumoured to be riddled with cellars, priest holes and secret passages; it is also said to be haunted.

St Michael's Church, Wentnor, *c.* 1910. The village lies on a high ridge on the opposite side of the Long Mynd to Little Stretton, between the River East Onny and the Criftin brook. St Michael's was rebuilt in 1885 by Sir Henry Curzon who re-used a great deal of the original Norman masonry and perpendicular roof. Inside the church is the Hurricane Stone, a memorial to a family who died when their home at the side of the Long Mynd was buried in an avalanche. Black Graves and Groaning Style are situated on the edge of the village, and are reputed to be where the people who died during the plague are buried.

Lydham Manor, Lydham, *c*. 1930. Lydham lies just 3 miles south-east of Bishop's Castle. Part of the parish lies within Shropshire, while part lies over the border in Powys. The old Manor was demolished in 1968 and the stable block was converted into a house. Within the park grows an old oak tree, the largest in the county and the second largest in Britain. The Lydham Oak has a girth which measures over 36 ft.

Linley Hall, More, *c*. 1930. The Hall was built by Henry Joynes of London for Sir Robert More MP in 1742. It's a square, stone Palladian-style mansion. The old timber-framed hall stood in front of the present building at the edge of the lake. Sir Robert More was a keen botanist and a friend of Linnaeus. He is reputed to have planted the first larch tree in England in the grounds of Linley Hall in 1783, on the same day that a similar tree was introduced at Dunkeld in Scotland.

Lydbury North, *c.* 1930. This village was a thriving centre of trade before Bishop's Castle, just 3 miles to the south-east, was founded. The name Lydbury means the fort on the slope, and there are traces of earthworks in the village. The church is dedicated to St Michael; it has two long transepts, which are known as the Walcot Chapel and the Plowden Chapel (which is Roman Catholic).

Lydbury North School, *c.* 1910. There were two schools in the village, one Catholic and one Church of England. The Church of England school was founded over 300 years ago by the Walcot family in a room over their chapel in the church. A new school was built in 1845 to hold 170 children. It was supported by an endowment of £16 a year and by voluntary contributions. The Catholic school was erected in 1874 and enlarged in 1896; the Plowden family supported it for many years.

The Bog Mine, *c.* 1910. The mine was first recorded in about 1739. At the end of the nineteenth century only nine men were employed at the mine producing lead, zinc ore and barytes. In 1910 the mine was taken over by Shropshire Mines Ltd, who took the work force up to 100. The Ramsden Shaft was sunk and the first electric winding gear in Shropshire was installed in 1915. Behind the buildings on the right is the winding gear of the Bunting shaft. Towards the end of its life most of the work was done from this shaft and the main product was barytes. The mine ceased production in 1924. The Bunting winding gear remained *in situ* until about 1960 and the buildings were demolished in the 1970s. Today visitors can learn about the area's mining heritage from a series of information boards on the site.

Crowsnest Dingle, *c.* 1905. Dingle is a local name for a valley. The Cross Guns Inn occupied the white building from about 1838 until the early 1930s. In 1901 the owner was the Marquess of Bath. The accommodation at this time consisted of a kitchen, a bar, a parlour, two bedrooms, a back kitchen and a cellar. At the rear of the building was a clubhouse, which had a billiard table, and where dances were held and dance lessons given. The last landlord was William John Salter.

Pennerley, *c.* 1910. The village was once a very busy mining settlement with its own public house called the Crown. The Earl of Tankerville once owned the land and lead was mined there from about 1780. The mine was run jointly with the Bog Mine.

The Devil's Chair and Window, *c.* 1890. The Devil's Chair is the highest and largest of the six outcrops of quartzite rock that run along the ridge of the Stiperstones. Legends abound in the area: if the rocks are shrouded in mist the Devil is sitting on his chair; another tale is that if the rocks ever sink back into the earth it will be the end of the world, so the Devil sits on the rocks, using his considerable weight to try and push them back into the ground. The window was caused by a piece of rock resting between two other stones; unfortunately it fell down some years ago.

Snailbeach, *c.* 1920. Snailbeach was once described as one of the most important lead mines in the kingdom. The Romans were the first to work the outcrops of ore, but it wasn't until the eighteenth century that the rich Snailbeach vein was fully exploited. By the middle of the nineteenth century 500 men were working at the mine and around 3,500 tons of ore were produced annually. Although mining in the area ceased in 1955 and the population dwindled, a great deal remains to remind the visitor of former times.

Snailbeach Mine, *c.* 1900. This view looking west shows great industrial activity. On the left is the Snailbeach Narrow Gauge Railway. Just 2 ft 4 in wide and around 3 miles long, it was opened in 1877 and connected the mine to the Pontesbury Sidings. The line can also be seen on the right between the white building and Black Tom Shaft winding gear; the shaft was sunk in 1820. The building with the two gable ends in the centre is the loco shed; to the left of that are the new crusher and compressor houses.

The Cosy Café, Snailbeach, *c.* 1935. The café was run by Miss Mary Ann Wardman who was known locally as Molly. She also ran a small shop that sold almost everything you would need. The café was situated in an army-style hut with a round corrugated metal roof. There you could order a pot of tea, jam sandwiches and cakes, but regulars remember that nothing was ever hot!

Postman Thomas Williams, *c.* 1910. Mr Williams' mail round stretched from Minsterley to the Bog. He carried out his duties for thirty-three years, without ever having a holiday, with no time off through ill health and even working on Christmas Day. It was estimated that he had walked over 165,000 miles during his career.

The Stiperstones, *c.* 1920. This range of hills is now a National Nature Reserve and lies across a valley to the west of the Long Mynd. The name Stiperstones is derived from 'stripped stone', the hill being a long ridge with several outcrops of quartzite rock, caused by frost during the last Ice Age. The highest point is the Devil's Chair. The other outcrops are Shepherd's Rock to the north and Manstone and Cranberry Rocks to the south.

The Roundhill Mine, *c.* 1910, which was about a mile east-north-east of Shelve. It began extracting lead ore in the middle of the nineteenth century, but production was never large: the total output of lead ore between 1863 and 1913 was only 3,038 tons. It opened and closed several times in the early part of the twentieth century. The steam engine at this mine was manufactured at the Perran Foundry, Falmouth in 1874.

Worthen Village Hall, c. 1975. This photograph was taken during the finals of the Shropshire Village Venture Competition. Dr Tim Watson expounds on the features of his new surgery in the village hall to the panel of judges. Left to right: Paul Roberts, former Chairman of the Village Hall Committee; Brian Holmes of Shell, judge; Ray Nunn, Chief Officer for the Community Council of Shropshire; Maureen Knight of Shell; County Council Chairman Reggie Lloyd, judge; Dr Watson; Kathy Dugdale, Chair of the Community Council of Shropshire, judge.

Chirbury, c. 1935. The village lies right on the border of England and Wales. St Michael's Church, on the right behind the tree, stands on the site of an Augustinian priory. According to local folklore, if you walk twelve times around the church at twelve o'clock on Halloween you will hear the names of those in the village who will die during the next twelve months. The Herbert Arms Inn is named after Lord Herbert, first Lord of Chirbury in 1629. He left a valuable collection of chained books in the old School House. They are now preserved in the county's archives.

ACKNOWLEDGEMENTS

I am indebted to so many people who have loaned me photographs and postcards of South Shropshire to enable me to write this book. I have been given unlimited access to three large collections. The first of these was the photographic library of the *Shropshire Star*, who have done a wonderful job recording news and events in our county since 1963. The second source is Ray Tipton, who loaned me his very large and comprehensive collection of postcards of the Stretton area. The third person is Denis Sherwood, whose family photographs and postcards of the Clun area make up a wonderful collection. For their kindness I am most grateful.

I would also like to thank the following people for their kindness and generosity in trusting me with their photographic treasures, which have been used in this book: Abbeycolor, David and Elizabeth Benson, Mr and Mrs Davies, the late Len Davies BEM, Ron Farr for his mother's collection, the late Mrs Olive Farr, Greenhous Shrewsbury Ltd, Christine Harvey, Ursula Penny, Roy Pilsbury, Ann Power, Mrs E. Ruscoe, H.R. 'Jim' Savage, David and Jean Woodhouse.

I would also like to thank Tony Carr and all the staff at the Shropshire Records and Research Centre for their help. I would like to acknowledge the help I received from articles written in the *Shropshire Star* by Toby Neil, who has done a great deal recently to reveal our county's interesting past. I am also grateful to Robert Evans of Abbeycolor for his continuing help, advice and expertise in preparing the photographs for this publication.

BIBLIOGRAPHY

Balwin, M., *Cleobury 2000*, M. & M. Balwin, 1999
Bilbey, D., *A History of Church Stretton*, Phillimore & Co. 1985
Lloyd, D., *A Concise History of Ludlow*, Merlin Unwin, 1999
——, *Ludlow*, Chalford, 1995
Lloyd, D. & Thomas, G., *Ludlow: A Second Selection*, Chalford, 2000
Meech, J., *Shropshire Towns and Villages*, Sigma Leisure, 2000
Moore, R.K., *Memories of Clun*, Shropshire Libraries, 1986
Bucknall in View, Pentabus, *c.* 1985
Preshous, J., *Bishop's Castle Well Remembered*, 2nd edition, 1995
Raven, M., *The Shropshire Gazeteer*, M. Raven, 1989
Shropshire Country guide, Shropshire County Council, 1988
Shropshire WI, *The Shropshire Village Book*, Countryside Books, 1988
——, *Shropshire Within Living Memory*, Countryside Books, 1988
The Victoria History of Shropshire, vol 10, Oxford University Press